PRAISE FOR

WHAT THE CORPSE REVEALED

"An entertaining primer on how these modern-day Sherlock Holmeses crack even the toughest cases."
—*Boston Phoenix*

"This well-written book holds the reader's attention through all the backgrounds and method of forensic detection. The reader will be amazed how far forensic science has come in helping to finish the story. Strongly recommended."
—*Library Journal*

"Miller's mastery of the alternately grisly and frustratingly arcane science of forensic criminology is admirable, and his presentation of this potentially obscure material is lucid and informative."
—*Kirkus Reviews*

WHAT THE CORPSE REVEALED

MURDER AND THE SCIENCE OF FORENSIC DETECTION

HUGH MILLER

St. Martin's Paperbacks

First published in Great Britain by Headline Book Publishing, a division of Hodder Headline PLC, under the title *Forensic Fingerprints: Remarkable Real-Life Murder Cases Solved by Forensic Detection*.

WHAT THE CORPSE REVEALED: MURDER AND THE SCIENCE OF FORENSIC DETECTION

Library of Congress Catalog Card Number: 99-20223

ISBN: 0-312-97573-2

Printed in the United States of America

St. Martin's Press hardcover edition / June 1999
St. Martin's Paperbacks edition / December 2000

St. Martin's Paperbacks are published by St. Martin's Press, 175 Fifth Avenue, New York, N.Y. 10010.

10 9 8 7 6 5 4 3

For Nettie,
as ever

CONTENTS

ACKNOWLEDGEMENTS

My thanks to Claire Halton and Lonnie James in Los Angeles, Charlie Spier in Amsterdam, Dr. Juan Aldecoa in Madrid, Dr. Palmira Adán in Barcelona, Tim Conroy in Berlin and the amazing Professor Joe Temple, who still gets everywhere.

I am especially grateful to Gustavo Rivero, Emilio Olivares, Tina Morton and Matt Hackett for photographs and taped interviews.

To Janice, Eric and Gail I am more indebted than I can say.

PREFACE

A forensic pathologist was gracious enough to say he liked my first collection of criminal cases solved by forensic scientists, but he added, "They're very spectacular—not at all like the stuff I deal with most of the time."

Quite so. Two criteria governed the selection of material for this collection: the investigations had to be solved chiefly through the efforts of forensic scientists, and the cases—as presented in this book—had to be exceptional enough to hold a reader's attention.

Cases handled by forensic scientists are usually anything but spectacular, but the description of colourless routine has no power to divert; and that, plain and simple, is the purpose of this volume—to divert the reader. A casualty department isn't quite the center of high drama this book might appear to suggest.

While all of the cases described in this book are inspired by actual events, the names of the characters, places and certain incidents and photographs portrayed in the book have been changed and/or fictionalized.

The forensic details, however, are genuine—they tell the stories of what real men in white coats did to solve difficult criminal cases. Here is a collection of engrossing criminal investigations inspired by actual events which reveal how, with considerable skill and ingenuity, forensic scientists cleared up mysteries and helped catch felons. They are anything but colourless.

NOTE TO THE READER

This book is inspired by actual events. However, the names of characters and places have been changed and certain characters, places, and events are the products of the author's imagination and/or have been fictionalized. This book is not intended to portray, and should not be read as portraying, actual persons, living or dead.

WHAT THE CORPSE
REVEALED

ONE

GAMBLER

On the morning of Monday 10 March, 1986, the body of Harry Brownlow was taken to the general hospital at Buenos Aires from his home at Quilmes, 15 kilometres south of the city. Harry was declared dead on arrival and the body was transferred to the mortuary in the hospital basement. Shortly after noon a pathologist, Dr. Andreas Peruna, examined the corpse and decided an autopsy would be in order.

"It had been four years since the conflict in the Falklands," said Peruna, "but there was still lingering ill-feeling in Argentina. In Buenos Aires anti-British slogans were still being chalked up on walls in the city centre. The unexplained death of an Englishman, right in our midst, could be a political hot potato. It was decided therefore that in determining a cause of death, we should go through all the proper procedures, with full publicity."

Harry Brownlow was born in London but was in fact an American citizen, having taken U.S. nationality in 1976. For two years until his death at the age of 42, he worked as a senior electrical maintenance engineer for the American co-owners of a meat, fish and grain processing business occupying a sprawling factory complex along the estuary on the eastern side of Buenos Aires.

By all accounts, Harry and his wife Beatrice had enjoyed living in Argentina. The house provided for them at Quilmes had every up-to-date convenience and all the latest gadgets; according to Beatrice it was a virtual replica of the home they had left behind in California.

"The company thought a lot of Harry," Beatrice said, "and they showed it every way they could. He was a valued asset and a very popular member of the technical support team. When he died his colleagues were devastated."

Beatrice had found Harry in his den at 8:30am that Monday morning, after believing he had left early for the plant without waking her. He was seated at his desk, his head resting on his arms. "He looked very peaceful and at first I thought he was asleep."

Part of the illusion of natural sleep was created by the appearance of Harry's skin: it was a healthy shade of pink, with deeper pink patches at the cheekbones.

"He looked as if he had just taken a good brisk walk," Beatrice said. "But when I touched his hand it was stone cold. The doctors told me later that by the time I found him, he had been dead several hours."

Dr. Peruna was sure of the cause of death even before he applied for permission to perform an autopsy: "The pink colour of the face and similar patchy coloration on other parts of the body told me the man had died of carbon monoxide poisoning."

Carbon monoxide is responsible for one of the commonest forms of lethal accidental poisoning in the developed world. The colourless, odourless gas causes death in two ways. First, because it has a 300-times greater ability than oxygen to mix with the haemoglobin in red blood cells, it can easily starve the body's tissues of oxygen by invading the space in the red cells normally occupied by oxygen. Second, carbon monoxide can dissolve in plasma, which is the liquid component of the blood, and so it can have a directly poisonous effect on the body cells supplied by the blood.

"The autopsy clinched it," said Dr. Peruna. "The blood was a bright red, the lungs were congested and puffy, with pinkish frothy fluid in the upper air passages. There were tiny haemorrhages on the surface of the brain—all of those and several other signs were entirely consistent with carbon monoxide poisoning. A blood sample analysis showed a 52 per cent saturation of carbon monoxide in the haemoglobin."

So, there was no doubt what had killed Harry Brownlow, but his death was nevertheless an intriguing mystery. Carbon monoxide is produced in several ways: by coal-gas, which is hardly ever encountered nowadays; by motorvehicle exhaust fumes; by coke ovens, blast furnaces and other industrial installations; by faulty domestic gas appliances. Harry had died at home, in his own den, where there were no devices or installations capable of producing carbon monoxide.

"It wasn't a case of the body having been moved after death, either," said Inspector Juan Galdós, a senior investigating officer. "Dr. Peruna made a careful check of the hypostasis on the body. It was practically the first thing he did."

When death occurs the blood circulation stops at once. The veins and arteries relax and let the blood flow downwards by gravity, where it settles in the vessels of the lower parts of the body. This is referred to as hypostasis. Blood cannot flow into areas where the body is in contact with hard surfaces, such as chairs or floorboards; these areas are flattened and appear lighter in colour than the areas where blood has settled. If a body is moved after death its position is almost inevitably changed and a second set of visible margins is formed. The first set, however, does not disappear, so it is obvious even to a moderately trained observer that the body has been moved.

"Brownlow's body had not been moved," said Inspector Galdós. "He died where he was found."

It was impossible for the police to overlook the likelihood that Harry Brownlow had been murdered. "Suicide was a possibility too, of course," said Dr. Peruna, "but no one would have bet on that one."

To forestall a flurry of press speculation, the Argentinian authorities invited an American team to take charge of the investigation. Two NYPD Forensic Officers, Barry Clemens and Jack Dexter, accompanied detectives Howard Timms and Luke Harris to Buenos Aires. They were backed by a trio of policemen—officers Jay Bruce, Arthur Conroy and Pete Lewis—with specialised training and wide experience in crime-scene management and the collection of forensic specimens.

"We were given every co-operation," Clemens said. "Our HQ consisted of two very comfortable suites in a top-class hotel near the *Congreso Nacional*. We were also provided with office and laboratory facilities. I could tell the Argentinians were worried that one of their own had killed Harry Brownlow, but they were ready to face the consequences of that. There was no suggestion at any time that there would be a cover-up, whatever the outcome."

While the detectives began mapping the history of Harry Brownlow's professional and social life in Buenos Aires, Barry Clemens and Jack Dexter made a thorough forensic sweep of the room where Brownlow had died.

"It was a frustratingly negative exercise," Dexter said. "The room was a typical middle-class American male's den of the mid-80s, with all the toys and faintly macho trappings you would expect—early sports trophies, a more recent golf tournament cup, class photos, pictures taken on fishing and hunting trips, guns and knives mounted on display plaques, that kind of stuff. There was a lot of it, and to do the sweep justice we had to examine everything and do as much detailed sampling as the layout called for."

Officers Bruce, Conroy and Lewis helped with the examination of the den, and Barry Clemens made a comprehensive photographic record. "If we were going to go back to the States with zilch in the way of a solution to the mystery," he said, "I was determined our failure would be one of the best-dressed and most heavily documented of its kind."

They found nothing of any apparent significance. No enigmas turned up. The case was as plain as it was mysterious: Harry Brownlow had died in his chair behind his desk in his den; there had been no struggle, no disturbance, and the den contained no means of producing the carbon monoxide which had killed him.

"We went back and had a look at the body," Dexter said. "All it did was confirm the picture. The man had died in a sitting position. There were no marks of violence on his body and the hypostasis clearly indicated that after he died, he hadn't been moved until shortly after his wife found him."

Meanwhile, detectives Timms and Harris were assembling a comprehensive history of the final two years in Harry Brownlow's life. He and his wife had been socially active but the circle of their acquaintances was small, due to the difficulty of mingling freely with the Argentinians.

"The company had a policy on that," Timms said, "and Brownlow stuck by it. It was called Cautious Integration. The Brownlows would always accept first-time invitations, and if one of those happened to be to the home of an Argentinian, well fine. However, if there was any show of opposition or resentment during the visit, the Brownlows would stay polite, but they would never visit with those people or their friends again."

"What it boiled down to," Harris said, "was that after the first eight or nine months in Buenos Aires, they mostly mixed with other Americans. There was a house-party circuit, a kind of rotation, and they fell into that and stayed there. It seemed to work out fine. There were enough different people in the circuit to keep the social scene interesting and stimulating, and Harry enjoyed himself. Beatrice said she didn't enjoy it quite so much as he did, because most of the women were younger than she was, and she missed having conversations with women her own age, and with similar interests."

The fact that Beatrice was ten years older than Harry was not lost on the detectives, and they took the usual cynical investigative line of trying to find out if there were any other women in Harry's life.

"As far as we could discover at that point," Timms said, "he had been clean as a whistle. His American pals in Buenos Aires all told the same story, with only minor variations. Harry was a guy who liked his work, he enjoyed an after-hours beer and a few bourbons on weekends. He joked a lot and although he appeared as mentally promiscuous as the next man, he seemed to be devoted to his wife and never indicated that he'd cheated on her."

Clemens and Timms, frustrated by the absence of clues in their forensic search, had meanwhile decided to go back to the Brownlow house and carry out detailed sweeps of the living room, kitchen and bedrooms. Although these areas had already been examined, they had received much less serious attention than the den.

"This time," Clemens said, "we were determined that the intensive technique would take in the whole house. It wasn't the most sophisticated approach to take, since usually a forensic team will use some savvy to work out where they can most effectively concentrate their efforts, but here we had nothing, no line to follow and no clues to grab at. All we could do was eliminate and eliminate and hope that at the end of it all, something significant would be left poking up."

The second sweep, which in the end took in the living room, kitchen, bedrooms, basement, attic, garage and garden shed, proved every bit as negative as the search of the den.

Said Clemens, "We didn't even find an old oil heater, or anything else that could have remotely been the source of a lethal quantity of carbon monoxide. Before the search was over, I was already drafting my report in my head. It was rich with descriptive detail, sketches and tables, all of it adding up to the fact that we hadn't the first idea how Harry Brownlow had died the way he did."

At the end of the first week of the investigation, Jack Dexter went back to the den in the Brownlow house and tried, in his own words, "to psych myself into feeling the room the way Harry had." He needed to understand the room better, he believed, before he could say with certainty that it held no useful evidence.

"I sat down at the desk, I clasped my hands on the ornamental leather blotter cover, and I let myself be as receptive as I possibly could. I believe I stayed that way for several minutes. I'd like to say that it worked, that gradually I saw the room through new eyes, and was aware of significant shifts and changes in the way it was now. But that didn't happen."

What did happen was that Dexter found himself staring at a box of playing cards on the desk. It had already been examined, along with everything else on the desktop, but Dexter opened it and began shuffling one of the two packs inside.

"All I was doing, I suppose, was trying to relax myself a little more, feeling the cards flowing through my hands, enjoying the tactile business of riffling, cutting and shuffling."

Then he noticed something unusual. As he riffled one end of the deck of cards, the back design appeared to have independent movement. At the left side of the upper narrow edge, white flecks seemed to move across the pattern as he riffled.

"A bell rang," Dexter said. "This was familiar. I hadn't seen it before but I had been told about it, by an old guy who once worked on the bunko squad just after the Second World War. I turned the pack round and riffled the other end. The same thing happened;

little dots of white seemed to jiggle back and forward
on the printed design on the back of the cards."

The cards were marked. Each one had been treated
with a sharp-pointed instrument to remove two tiny
parts of the design. The result was that two small areas of white appeared on each card. One mark indicated the card's suit, the other denoted its value.
Because the marks appeared in different places on
every card, the white marks seemed to move about
when the cards were riffled.

"I looked at the other pack. They were marked, too.
Every one had been carefully treated to be readable
from its back. This wasn't exactly a breakthrough in
the case, but it was something unexpected, and that
got me all enthusiastic."

Dexter recalled seeing three or four packs of cards
in a drawer in the living room when the large-scale
search was being conducted. He got them now and
examined them. Sure enough, they were marked.

"Every deck of cards in the house was crooked.
That really was unusual. I didn't know what it meant,
but I decided I should find out."

Dexter alerted the detectives, Timms and Harris.
Timms said they would check out the possibility of a
gambling angle. Up to the time Dexter called, the detectives believed they knew everything there was to
know about Harry Brownlow. Being experienced detectives with no illusions about themselves, they did
not hesitate to accept that they could be wrong.

"And boy, were we wrong," said Luke Harris. "As
soon as we began asking Brownlow's friends about a

history of gambling, they went cagey on us. At first it was a lot of 'Well, I'm not sure about that,' or 'I can't say I recall any gambling,' and so forth, not very convincing and definitely vague. Then one of his buddies, another engineer at the meat plant, blew the whistle. He told us he had never gambled himself, he was a Christian and it was against his principles, but he had heard about regular card games over at Harry's place. It was always kind of hush-hush, he said, because there was serious money involved, and the company didn't approve of its employees getting involved in anything of that kind, especially not on a big scale."

The investigative team were on to something. They had no idea what it was—but it was something to follow and that made a change. Detective Timms carried out a background check on Brownlow, covering the five-year period before he had gone to work in Argentina. Detective Harris started questioning the friends and acquaintances again, this time leaning on them harder, insisting they tell him all they knew about the gambling.

The background checks threw up a picture of a different Harry Brownlow from the one they had already researched.

"He was a fully-trained engineer, time-served with all the correct certificates," said Timms, "but he also had a record of compulsive gambling from the age of 14. It wasn't the usual kind of compulsion—you know, betting on the nags, getting into dangerous poker games and losing more than he won, always short of cash because the habit was expensive, just like every addiction.

"This was very different. Brownlow's compulsion was to beat everybody else. He got an inordinate kick from making people lose to him at cards."

Standing-order mandates at Brownlow's home-base bank in California showed that he made regular annual membership payments to IBM—which turned out to be the International Brotherhood of Magicians, of which he had been a member since he was 16.

"I spoke on the telephone to several people in his local ring of the Brotherhood," said Harris, "and they each told me what a whiz Harry Brownlow had been with the pasteboards. He could second-deal, bottom-deal, palm and side-steal as easy as most people handle a knife and fork. He had even devised a method of removing cards from the pack, undetected, that he had published in one of the card experts' magazines."

While several people attested to Harry Brownlow's skill with cards, no one was able to say that he had ever been interested in card magic, or in conjuring of any kind.

"Technique had been his enthusiasm, exclusively," Harris said. "He only mixed with magicians to get to know their methods, so he could adapt them to his own purpose, which was to skin the hide off any sucker dumb enough to play cards with him."

Timms finally questioned Beatrice Brownlow about the card games at their house in Buenos Aires. He had held off from interviewing her until he had a good idea of the true scale and frequency of the games. At

first, Beatrice denied there had ever been gambling at
their house, or anywhere else they went. The packs
of playing cards, she said, were there because both
she and her husband had occasionally enjoyed playing
solitaire.

"I told her I had learned that there were often
games at her house, games where people sometimes
lost substantial sums of money. I also pointed out that
all the decks of cards at her house were marked. She
sat staring at her hands for a while, then she said OK,
it was true, Harry did have a thing about card games,
and he did usually win."

Beatrice said that although she had seen her husband working on playing cards with a knife, she had
not known the cards were marked—she had simply
not made the connection. Timms was inclined to believe her. On the whole, she gave the impression that
her husband's need to beat people had completely bewildered her. At ordinary times, she said, Harry was
as evenly balanced as any man could be. When he
gambled, though, he was ferocious. He took obvious
glee in winning, and he won so often that inevitably
there were those who believed he had to be cheating.
Some people fell out with Harry because of the card
games, but he would always take the trouble to woo
them round again, apologising for the rabid nature of
his enthusiasm and promising that in future he would
try to curb his zeal.

"By now, the detectives had a theory going," Barry
Clemens said. "It wasn't one they could believe in

wholeheartedly, but like the discovery of the marked cards, it was something to follow."

The tentative assumption was that somebody had become so angry about losing money to the gloating Harry Brownlow that they had decided to wipe the glee off his face for good. This theory automatically placed most of Harry's friends and acquaintances in the category of suspects. The three police officers drafted in to help the forensic investigators were now re-assigned to the detectives to help question suspects.

"My colleague Jack Dexter had really started something with his discovery of the marked cards," said Barry Clemens. "We decided now, between us, that while the detectives were off following their vengeance theory, we would concentrate on the fine details of what little we had discovered so far. It's the experience of most seasoned workers in the field of scientific crime detection that the real answers are to be found in the details. Apart from that, we couldn't really think of what else we could do at that point."

Barry Clemens approached Beatrice Brownlow and asked her what kind of instrument her husband had used to work on the playing cards. She said it was something like a scalpel, a silver-coloured, shiny knife with a narrow pointed blade. Clemens asked her where Harry kept the scalpel, and she said probably in his safe.

"Safe?" Clemens said. "What safe?"

Beatrice shrugged. She didn't know where the safe was, but she knew there was one. It was the same place he kept his winnings from the gambling. There had been a key, she said, but she didn't know where Harry kept it—although she believed it might be under the rectangle of Persian carpet on which his desk stood. "I saw him on his hands and knees at the corner of the desk one night," she said, "and he had the key in his hand."

The rug had already been checked during the exhaustive sweep of the den; nothing had been found under it. However, something had clicked in Clemens's memory. The image of Harry Brownlow on his hands and knees at the corner of the desk made Clemens think of a security ploy he had seen at a house in New York. It was a hollowed out foot on a heavy desk, with a plug in the open end. The cavity of the wooden foot served as a perfect safe for storing small valuables.

Clemens went to the den again and got on his hands and knees by the desk at the place Beatrice had described seeing her husband. He lifted the front left corner of the desk and slipped his fingers under the short metal leg. Light pressure on the footplate made it slide aside. A key dropped into Clemens's hand.

"It was a well-cut steel key, obviously designed to open a serious lock. The trouble was, of course, that in all our exhaustive searching of the Brownlow home, we hadn't found anything remotely resembling a safe."

Clemens told Dexter about the key, and Dexter immediately suggested they have another look at Brownlow's office at the plant. The office had already been

searched routinely and nothing of importance had
been found.

"It was one of those offices without a trace of coloration from the occupant," Clemens said. "The first
time it was searched, we didn't find any personal
items at all, apart from a picture of Beatrice Brownlow in a frame on the desk."

"We searched the office again," Dexter said, "and
again we found nothing. But this time, because we
knew what we wanted to find, maybe we had stronger
motivation. Anyway, we made a third sweep of the
office, and this time we found the safe. It was built
into the margin of the floor between the inner office
and the computer room.

"The front of the safe was a strip of metal three
inches wide, and the steel body of the safe was fitted
into the floor like a drawer, two feet by two feet. The
keyhole was under a flush flap of metal, and the whole
thing lay under the point where the carpet of Brownlow's office butted against the carpet in the computer
room. When the door separating the rooms was
closed, the safe was inaccessible."

Inside the safe Clemens and Dexter found $24,000
in rubber-banded bundles. They also found the scalpel
used for marking the cards, a high-quality German
magnifying glass, six fresh packs of playing cards already marked, and an envelope containing three pictures of a young blonde woman in the nude.

"The money was no surprise," said Clemens, "and
neither were the cards or the scalpel. The pictures
were something of a bombshell, however—especially

since, on close examination, we were able to establish the extent of Brownlow's involvement with the girl. All three shots were probably taken at the same time, in a bedroom somewhere, and in one of them, there was an open wardrobe door with a mirror inside. Using the magnifier from the safe to examine the image we could clearly see the reflection of Harry Brownlow, as naked as the girl, pointing a camera at her. The camera was a Bronica with a waist-level finder, so there was nothing obscuring the photographer's face. The man was Brownlow all right."

But who was the woman? Clemens used a computer and a scanner to make a modified replica of one of the pictures, showing only the woman's head and shoulders. Several copies were produced and officers Bruce, Conroy and Lewis began discreet enquiries. Detectives Timms and Harris, having acknowledged that Clemens and Dexter had made the case their own, now took a voluntary background role and made themselves available to carry out any interrogation work that might, in time, become necessary.

"Officer Jay Bruce had the woman identified within an hour," Clemens said. "She was an American, Andrea Kelly, employed by the same company as Brownlow. She was part of a research team working on the development of new kinds of airtight packaging."

Dexter smiled when he recalled his immediate reaction to the news that Andrea Kelly worked on airtight packaging. "I got this image, straight away, of Harry Brownlow being passed through a vacuum chamber, having all his air sucked out. I'd been speculating, of course, that the mystery woman would probably have some connection with Harry's death, so I guess the image I got was inevitable."

Detectives Timms and Harris were brought up to date on the situation, but Clemens asked them to hold off from questioning Andrea Kelly until he and Dexter had examined her working environment. They obtained permission to visit the research facility during the night, when only security teams were on duty.

"Suddenly the case was beginning to look routine," Clemens said. "From being a complete mystery it had now turned—well, *almost* transparent. In Andrea Kelly's work-bay we found cylinders of carbon monoxide, and beside them specialised equipment for filling smaller, pocket-sized cylinders from the larger ones. The gas was used in combination with a flash-freezing process to render meat sterile before packaging. I went to the detectives with what we had and left the rest to them."

Andrea Kelly was taken in for questioning early the next morning. She resisted all suggestions that she had known Brownlow in anything but a professional capacity, and the detectives let her go on resisting, squandering her defensive energy until she was exhausted from countering the innuendoes.

"And then we hit her with the photographs," Timms said. "She buckled. It wasn't as if she didn't know they existed, it was just that she imagined we didn't know anything about them, because all we did for a couple of hours was behave like we were acting on vague rumours."

"One look at the shots and she went to pieces," Detective Harris said. "For a while she was all babble. She said he had promised her this and that, like he would divorce his wife and they would get married, and she'd always been there for him, ready to slip off to a motel, or let him come out to her place, and then, bolt from the blue, he tells her it's over."

The reason for the split, Andrea told the detectives, was tied into Brownlow's obsession with winning. There had been a steep decline in his talent as a gambler—or, more accurately, as a successful card cheat. It was something, he said, that he couldn't overlook. Try as he might, he just couldn't get back the dominant form he had enjoyed before.

"The fact was," Timms said, "Brownlow was a lousy card player, and lately he had been trying his scam on people with the ability to win in spite of card-marking and second-dealing and all the other palaver."

Brownlow believed the start of his declining ability was at approximately the time he had promised Andrea he would divorce his wife. "He was superstitious," Andrea told the detectives. "He truly believed he had jinxed himself by promising to leave the woman who had been with him since he started out fleecing his guests at cards. And it was all-important to him; he just couldn't let himself lose the regular kicks he got, cheating people out of their money, even though he didn't need it."

Confessing his trickery to Andrea had been another mistake, in Brownlow's own estimation. He couldn't help bragging, he told her, because as the years had passed he had wanted to tell someone, but it had somehow never seemed right that he should let Beatrice in on his secret.

"So all his troubles were down to me," Andrea told the detectives. "The cure, as he saw it, was to ditch me."

"And he couldn't have chosen a worse woman to try it on," Timms said. "Andrea had a history of personality disturbance, and it was a lot worse than her doctors had ever figured. She told us that she knew the amazingly potent properties of carbon monoxide because she had used it on mice, rats and even a couple of domestic cats. This was one disturbed lady although, like a lot of them, she was very good at hiding it."

"When Brownlow dropped the bombshell on her," Harris said, "she went batshit. When the pain of it subsided, all she could think about was getting back at him."

"I gave it a lot of thought," she told the detectives. "In the end I decided he deserved to die. I didn't want to get caught, though, so I decided the best way to do it was in his own house, where no outside people could come under suspicion."

Andrea knew that Beatrice used sleeping pills and that she slept very soundly—she had even slept through a car bomb explosion at the end of the street during their first month in Buenos Aires. Andrea also knew that it was Harry Brownlow's practice, late on a Sunday evening, to sit in his den and review his work schedule for the coming week.

"So I called on Harry that Sunday evening. I decided that if my ringing the bell disturbed his wife, then I would tell her everything and leave it at that—she would have given him a very hard time, I'm sure—but mostly, I wanted to get into the house without disturbing Beatrice and then kill that bastard."

In her purse that night Andrea carried a miniature cylinder filled with pressurised carbon monoxide. She walked through the back streets to the Brownlow house, rang the bell, and waited.

"Harry opened the door. He was shocked to see me there. I asked if I could come in. I kept it quiet, civilised, I didn't want him to think I was out to make trouble. He invited me in and we went to the den. He sat down at the desk and I stood opposite. He told me to sit down. I didn't. Instead, I opened my purse, fumbled around for a second, then I brought out the cylinder of gas. I held it out in front of him and squirted it in his face. He inhaled a couple of times as he jerked back, and that was that. He went out. His eyes rolled back and I could see he was dead. I eased his arms on to the desk, laid his head down on the folded arms, and then I left the house."

Andrea had worn gloves, and her rubber-soled shoes were of a kind more likely to lift debris than deposit any. She left no significant trace of herself that night, and in the ordinary run of events, Detective Timms believed, she would never have been caught.

"She was sentenced to life for premeditated murder," he said. "After sentencing, the judge made a point of commending the forensic team for what he called 'uncommon assiduity' in cracking the case."

"It all hinged on Jack Dexter picking up that deck of cards," said Detective Harris. "If he hadn't got an attack of restless fingers, the case would have got buried and Andrea would still be a free woman, at liberty to gas any guy that crossed her."

TWO

THE PAIN OF LOSS

For thirty-two years the Washington, DC, law practice of Edgar Quintana thrived on copyright infringement suits and a steady flow of contract-drafting commissions. Then, on the last day of April 1992, a well-to-do Italian restaurateur from New York, Domenico Rossi, came to the office with a different kind of case. He asked to speak to Edgar Quintana in person.

"He told me his wife had left him," Quintana said. "I told him tough, so had mine. It's a hard thing to live with, I said, but we don't do missing-persons work. Rossi said he was there because he wanted me to prove that his wife, Giuseppina, known as Josie, was dead. Murdered, in fact. Killed by the man she had run away with three weeks before."

Quintana explained it was not a lawyer's job to set up a murder investigation. He said Rossi should go to the police. Rossi said no, he didn't trust policemen. He didn't trust lawyers either, especially not Italian ones, with so many of them steeped in deals with the Mafia and servicing crooked politicians.

"His dislike of lawyers was bolstered with a lot of standard prejudices," Quintana said, "but its roots lay in a big loss he took when he was starting out in business. Three customers at his first restaurant got food poisoning from their steaks. They sued Rossi for a total of a hundred thousand dollars, which was a lot back then. Rossi was told he could recoup his loss by suing the big meat-supply outfit that sold him the steaks. So he did that. The meat company responded by hiring an Italian shyster who not only convinced the court that it was innocent, but got Rossi declared negligent under the terms of the FDA regulations on the handling of raw beef. He had to pay the meat company's legal costs—thirty thousand—and cough up a fine of fifty thousand when the FDA prosecuted him."

In spite of the traumatic history, Rossi was prepared to trust Quintana.

"He told me his wife had gone away with an attorney, an employee at the Democratic Party Headquarters in Manhattan. As far as Rossi was concerned, any enquiries he made on his own behalf would be torpedoed by corrupt lawyers and shady politicos protecting their own."

Quintana asked Rossi why he had come to him, of

all the lawyers he might have approached. Rossi said he had been told Quintana was an honest man, one who always put his client's interests first. The person who had told Rossi this was Russell Carney, a journalist on a Washington newspaper who often dined at Rossi's New York restaurant. Later he told Quintana why he had recommended him.

"He explained he was a Washington old-hand," Quintana said. "He'd watched how my dad, a Mexican immigrant, stood up to the cops, to the business bullies, and the shits on Nob Hill. He watched how the old man paddled his own canoe year after year until he'd established a solid law practice. It was a pleasure, Carney said, to put business the way of an outfit that was built on old-fashioned balls."

Quintana was flattered and felt glad that he had taken the commission. He had taken it, in the end, because it was a refreshing challenge, and because Rossi was obviously able to pay whatever it would cost.

"What Domenico Rossi wanted me to do was assemble the proof that his wife had been unlawfully killed, and that her killer was Brian Hopkins, a 35-year-old attorney. First I had to know what made Rossi so sure his wife was dead."

Rossi said there were two reasons. First, his wife was a creature of near-compulsive habits, one of which was to call her mother in New Jersey every morning at ten o'clock.

"She never failed, not since she left home at age eighteen," he said. "All through her six years working in New York, and later, during the eight years of our marriage, every morning you could guarantee she'd call the old lady. They would talk for a few minutes and that would be that, but it never varied, seven times a week, every week. But four days after she left me the calls to her Momma stopped."

There was another reason he believed Josie was dead. In 1993 she had been diagnosed as diabetic. Her diabetes was of the non-insulin dependent type, and her treatment regime had been a careful diet plus daily doses of the drug tolbutamide. When Josie left her husband she had only eight tablets, a four-day supply, and her doctor had not issued a fresh prescription.

"I monitored her pills," Rossi explained. "For somebody strict in her habits, Josie was lax about medication, so I always made a point of reminding her. This drug, you see, tolbutamide, it's a compound that causes a decrease in blood sugar. So it was very, very important that she have it regularly, otherwise her sugar levels would go way up and the consequences of that, for a diabetic, could be disastrous. When she left I called her doctor to ask if she'd had a new prescription. He said no. I asked him how long she could handle things when the stuff ran out. He said she couldn't go more than a week without her drug. She would get very sick."

To Edgar Quintana none of this suggested that Josie was dead. He could think of believable alternatives, one of them being that Josie had made a clean break with her old life, which included her slavish contact with her mother, and had found it easy to locate a doctor who would prescribe for her condition. Rossi, however, would accept none of that. He was certain his wife had been murdered.

"I have the circumstantial facts to tell me," he said, "and I have the pain of loss to convince me." He wanted it proved and he wanted her killer brought to justice.

Quintana hired John Luce, a successful New York private investigator, and told him to find out all he could about Josie and her lover. Luce was a former NYPD detective, invalided out of the force after a shooting incident in which he lost an eye. He enjoyed a good relationship with his former colleagues and, unlike most other PIs, he could count on police co-operation with his enquiries.

"Luce had a reputation for being a flamboyant, daredevil kind of operator," said Quintana, "but he was a hard worker, too, with a sound track record. Two days after being hired he was back with the goods."

It transpired that Josie's affair with Brian Hopkins hadn't been discreet. Acquaintances on both sides knew they were lovers. They were seen together at restaurants and clubs for six or seven weeks before Josie finally left her husband, and their public displays of affection left no doubt about the nature of their feelings for each other.

"Among friends the consensus was that they were a really odd couple," Quintana said. "They were completely unalike in background, temperament, culture.

Worlds apart, in fact, except they had the hots for each other."

Josie was 34, a former secretary at Democratic Headquarters who met Brian Hopkins one evening when he visited Rossi's restaurant with Josie's former boss. Hopkins and Josie were introduced by Rossi himself, who happened to be dining with Josie in the restaurant that night.

"It seems that Josie and Brian clicked straight away," Quintana said. "No preliminaries worth talking about. Within the week, according to two witnesses, they were spending afternoons in Brian Hopkins's apartment."

It took John Luce only a short time to discover that Josie had been unusually promiscuous since the age of 16, a fact which seemed to have eluded her husband. The stories of Josie's adventures, up to and beyond the time she married Domenico Rossi, created a picture of a woman with no capacity for loyalty who would make a pass at any man who attracted her.

Luce turned up numerous instances of Josie's wild behaviour.

"Her one-time best friend, Lily Conroy, took a kind of grim satisfaction telling me about the time Josie got caught having sex in a movie house with her— Lily's—boyfriend. The theatre management were having a lot of that kind of trouble at the time, so they needed to make an example of somebody, and Josie was it. They tried to bring a suit against her and the boy for lewd behaviour. The thing never got to court, but it blew up a whole lot of embarrassing publicity, enough to drive the boyfriend away to another town and stop Josie and her family from showing up in daylight for quite a time."

Luce also obtained evidence that showed Josie could be uncommonly possessive.

"There had been some nasty scenes in the past. One time she was caught at two in the morning, lurking in the garden of a married man who had ditched her. Another time she followed a couple into a restaurant and sat at a table near theirs, just staring at the man. The management had to call the police to get her removed."

As far as Luce could determine, Josie's colourful history ended on Sunday 12 April, 1992. At approximately 11 o'clock that morning an acquaintance saw her get out of a taxi in front of Brian Hopkins's apartment building. Hopkins refused to speak to John Luce and threatened that if he persisted in trying to ask questions, he would be landed with a suit for harassment. Quintana urged Luce to try harder.

"And that was where Luce's famed daredevil streak came into play," Quintana said. "He got an actor friend of his to call on Brian Hopkins, passing himself off as a field operative of the FBI. I would have fainted at the thought of anyone pulling a stunt like that on my behalf, but when it was handed to me as a *fait accompli*, I have to admit I was amused. Hopkins caved in at the idea of the Feds being on his case and he talked to the actor for nearly an hour."

Hopkins told his visitor that on his birthday, Monday 30 March, he had split with Josie after they had

argued about her jealousy and her insistence on being
with him any time he was free.

"She came here with this expensive gift for me.
Monogrammed cufflinks. I refused to take them. I was
determined my birthday would be a day of big
changes, so in spite of the show of affection and the
gift, we had a fight, a wing-dinger, which I engineered. In the end I said I didn't want to see her any
more and she stormed out of here. I have no idea
where she went, and I swear I haven't seen her since."

The alleged break-up had taken place roughly four
weeks before Josie finally left her husband. When
Brian Hopkins was asked how he explained Josie being seen outside his apartment building on 12 April,
three days *after* she had left Rossi, he said he couldn't
explain that. He could only assume it was a case of
mistaken identity.

Quintana now began to think that Brian Hopkins
had killed Josie. He declared his suspicion in his second weekly report to Domenico Rossi and said it
would be sensible now to call in the police. Rossi said
no. He reminded Quintana of their arrangement: "You
bring me the proof, I'll decide what to do with it."

It dawned on Quintana that Rossi's refusal to deal
with the police, or with anyone in New York connected with the law, had nothing to do with distrust.
He wanted guilt to be proved before he administered
justice himself, on his own terms.

"It's something that happens more than you'd
think," Quintana said. "Guys, women too, will spend
lots of money getting proof-positive that some specific

person has done some specific dirt, then they pay off the lawyer, pick up the hatchet and cut themselves some justice."

During the third week of investigation John Luce had a breakthrough. One of his police contacts had been checking for stolen cars in the car park under Hopkins's apartment building when a security guard approached him.

"He told the officer he believed something bad had happened to a girl who had been visiting there in recent weeks," Quintana said. "This was a cranky old man close to retirement, suspicious of everything, but the officer knew about John Luce's investigation so he listened to what he had to say."

The guard told the police officer that the young woman had gone into the apartment block one day and had not come out again. "But he didn't mean Hopkins's block," Quintana said. "He meant the one adjoining. They shared the same car parking space."

The police officer pressed the guard to think hard. Did he really mean the missing girl had gone into the other building?

"The guard was absolutely certain of his facts," Quintana said. "Later, he identified Josie from a whole batch of pictures. He had watched her just as he watched the movements of other visitors. She had begun visiting on 10 April, which was the day after she left her husband."

On 16 April, when the attendant noticed Josie hadn't come out of the block, he checked with the security videos which recorded comings and goings in the foyer and the car park.

At 9:18 on 16 April, Josie had gone into the building and taken the elevator to the fourth floor. She did not appear on the tapes again. The guard knew about the high social standing of a lot of the residents in the block and he had no wish to bring trouble down on himself, especially not the kind that could cost him his pension. So he tried hard not to give voice to his suspicions, but silence began to play on his conscience, and when he saw the officer in the car park he decided to tell him what he knew.

This was a move forward, but it didn't give Luce a case to pursue. He decided, in the absence of any better idea, to put three assistants on door-to-door calls around the apartment block next to Hopkins's, in the hope of gaining eye-witness detail on Josie's last visit there.

The first day's calls produced no response. On the second afternoon an assistant rang the bell at apartment 419 and got surprise information from Iris Culp, an old lady who lived there alone. Sure, Iris said, she had seen the girl in the picture. Iris watched people through the spy-lens fitted to her door, and several times she had seen a man let Josie into apartment 420, directly opposite.

"He's a nice man, he's quiet and he keeps himself to himself. For a while, the young woman seemed to visit him every day. She usually stayed about an hour."

The last time Iris saw Josie leave the apartment she

looked flushed, and she had been crying. Next morning she was back, and the man let her in.

"I didn't ever see her again, and I didn't see her leave that day," Iris said, "although of course, she must have."

Now that Luce had something resembling a lead, he followed it. He learned that the man in apartment 420 was Bud McCowan, a statistician with a Manhattan advertising agency. McCowan was single and had lived in the apartment for three years. In an old address book of Josie's she had written the name Bud McCowan, but the address at that time had been in the Bronx. Later, it would transpire that they had once worked together in a law office and had been lovers for ten months.

"At the time Iris Culp spoke to the interviewer," Quintana said, "McCowan had just left on an eight-week business trip to Latin America. Luce didn't hesitate on the next move. Within three hours of knowing McCowan was out of the country, he and two of his helpers were inside apartment 420. Before they went in, Luce had a pow-wow with the NYPD Forensic Medical Department, so he would know what he was looking for."

Luce and his assistants spent two and a half hours combing the apartment, equipped with tweezers, low-tack tape, dust lifters, sterile swabs, specimen tubes and most of the other aids to evidence-gathering, including rubber-toothed forceps and suction bottles.

"Specimens of hair matched samples supplied from Josie's hairbrush. Fingerprints lifted from tables, a chairback and a window ledge were a match for Josie's prints, which were on file with the NYPD in connection with traffic violations when she was a teenager. In short, the evidence showed Josie had recently been in McCowan's apartment—but evidence was all there was. There was no trace of Josie."

During the process of fingerprint elimination, three samples caught the attention and interest of Homicide Division officers who were covertly in on the investigation. The prints belonged to two known murder victims, Mary Davis and Joanne Claven. Mary Davis's body had been found in an alley off a busy street six weeks before John Luce began his investigation into Josie Rossi's disappearance; the body of the other woman, Joanne Claven, had turned up in another alley two weeks later. Both women were call-girls, and both had been battered to death.

"The process of linking the dead women to Bud McCowan was set in motion," Quintana said, "and simultaneously the investigation became official. A forensic medical team entered the apartment and went to town on it."

Exhaustive enquiries within a two-mile radius of McCowan's apartment block finally uncovered the fact that he had contacted Mary Davis through a card she left in a telephone kiosk. McCowan kept an extensive library of recorded telephone conversations, going back over three years, and among them was the recording of his first approach to Davis, where he explained how he had come by her number.

"On that first occasion," Quintana said, "he didn't

actually make a date with her. Instead, he sounded her out on what she was prepared to do for her fee. She told him anything within reason. He responded by saying he particularly enjoyed carefully staged rituals of bondage and sexual degradation. That was OK by her, she said, and she even went on to ask him if he would prefer her to dress up in leather or rubber—she could provide either. He said he would get in touch."

When McCowan made his second call to Mary Davis he asked her to come to his apartment at eight that evening and to bring various items of fetishistic clothing. It was assumed and later proved that Mary Davis died before midnight on that date.

Some time after Mary Davis was murdered, McCowan picked up Joanne Claven in a singles bar, where prostitutes can usually do good business. The main witness to the pickup was a bartender. He watched the whole transaction and even listened in on McCowan's specification of the way he expected Claven to dress and perform.

"The barman was the last person known to have seen Joanne Claven alive," Quintana said. "When her body turned up, it was clear she had been the victim of severe torture. Cause of death was given as cardiac seizure, probably caused by the forced insertion of a wine bottle into her anus."

In the meantime forensic medical investigators were constructing a case fit to withstand the inevitable battering from an upmarket defence team. Scrapings of apocrine sweat taken from unlaundered bedclothes in one of McCowan's closets were found to be a genetic match for cell material taken from the body of Mary Davis.

"The sensitivity of the tests they conduct nowadays can be amazing," said Quintana. "They not only determined Davis had been rolling around on those sheets, they actually put a tentative date on the event."

Steven Mathias, a forensic biochemist involved in the case, said that every medico-legal investigator in the world gives thanks, at pretty regular intervals, for the body's natural tendency to plant traces of itself wherever it goes.

"Body sweat, especially the sweat of a naked body, leaves behind an identity record that can put a perpetrator or a victim—or both of them—at a particular place within a reasonably narrow time frame."

Mathias has made a speciality of identification through sweat deposits. "A person can soon learn to avoid leaving fingerprints," he said, "but unless you wrap up really snug and seam-free from head to toe in plastic, your chances of *not* leaving behind sweat deposits are zero."

Sweat glands, he explained, are found on all of the body's surfaces, except at the margin of the lips, on the glans penis and on the inner surface of the foreskin.

"The eccrine sweat gland is the commonest kind, covering most of the body's surface. The sweat it produces, which is practically odourless, regulates body temperature. When the internal temperature goes up, the eccrine glands transfer water to the surface of the skin, where the heat gets removed by evaporation."

Mathias went on to explain that traces of apocrine sweat, which proved that the call-girl Mary Davis had been in McCowan's apartment, usually carry more useful investigative information than the residues of eccrine sweat.

"Apocrine sweat glands are located in the armpits and pubic region," he said. "They open into hair follicles rather than directly on to the surface of the skin. They secrete a fatty sweat, and it's the action of local bacteria that gives the sweat its characteristic odour. The oiliness, plus the odour, can help advertise its presence on fabrics and furnishings at the scene of a crime."

Traces of other body secretions were used to substantiate the evidence that both Mary Davis and Joanne Claven had been in McCowan's apartment. Vaginal swabs from Joanne Claven matched deposits found on a plastic vibrator. Dried blood, saliva and nasal mucus on three cushions were genetic matches of material collected from both women's bodies.

"Two nasty murders were on the verge of being sewn up," Quintana said. "But as for Josie, we couldn't even prove she was dead."

No trace of Josie's body was ever found. McCowan eventually confessed to murdering the call-girls, he also volunteered a confession to another murder in New England in 1974. However, although he admitted inviting Josie into his apartment and admitted they had become lovers again on the day she broke up with Brian Hopkins, he said they decided they no longer had enough in common, and parted cordially. He denied harming her.

For Domenico Rossi, the legacy of a costly investigation was the tormenting uncertainty over what had happened to Josie. On top of that he had the pain of her infidelities, which inevitably came to light. Additionally, there was the frustration of having no one to blame for Josie's disappearance.

Throughout McCowan's trial on three counts of murder, Rossi tried to plead through Quintana for a clue to the whereabouts of his wife's body, but McCowan refused even to say she was dead.

Three months after Bud McCowan went to prison for life, Domenico Rossi died of a coronary attack. His heart, a friend said, simply could not sustain all the pain and misery.

"The payoff, if that's what it was," said Quintana, "was that in March 1993, two days before his birthday, Brian Hopkins took a deliberate overdose of barbiturate and died in the bathtub at his apartment. He left a note on the washbasin. It said, 'When the truth about Josie is known I may be forgiven, but I cannot forgive myself.' You have to wonder what Domenico Rossi would have made of that."

THREE

A DREAM OF POWER

In the old days the poisoners had it all their own way," said Jorge Perlosio, a senior toxicologist from Barcelona. "When I was a child, poisoning was a convenient way to get rid of someone. Poisoners were hardly ever convicted, because poisoning was a hard thing to prove, and the really accessible poisons were mostly unclassified."

Progress in chemistry, plus improvements in communications and scientific co-operation have made important changes. World centres for poisons research regularly update their computer records. They alert each other to new poisons and the increasingly subtle methods of administering them. Even so, fresh tragedies and grim comedies take place every day.

One of Jorge Perlosio's most memorable cases concerns a series of deaths of young women between 1990 and 1992, all of them occurring in resorts along the Costa del Sol in southern Spain.

"Every year many people die in those tourist places," said Perlosio. "Old age and ill-health figure strongly in the statistics. So does alcoholic poisoning. For a while the victims in this case were assumed to be fatalities of drink. They were young; they were country girls who had moved to the holiday resorts to make good money and to have a good time.

"Every year an average of twenty girls fitting that description will die in the resorts, usually from alcohol overdose. That is because they grow up without ever touching strong drink. They arrive on the Costa with livers and pancreatic systems too clean and tender to withstand the onslaught of hard liquor in large quantities."

Perlosio first noticed similarities in apparently random deaths when he began preparing figures for a paper he was writing on ethyl alcohol poisoning.

"The details came together very tidily, in a way that the computer could not ignore," he said. "Orderly results in such investigations are ridiculous, because there is no neatness or symmetry in the true statistics of sudden death."

Of twenty-two cases where the primary cause of death was given as alcoholic poisoning, eleven were young women between 18 and 22 who exhibited almost identical internal signs at autopsy. Nine doctors had conducted the autopsies at eight different locations, so in the ordinary run of events, close similarities would not have been noticed.

"And besides, alcoholic poisoning is such a common, unexceptional cause of debility and death in those parts," Perlosio said, "no one was alert even to the possibility of murder."

In the eleven suspect cases, the examining pathologists had noted yellowish or tan discoloration of the liver; histological analysis was carried out on all of the livers, and in each case there was a finding of centrilobular necrosis.

"In plain language," said Perlosio, "that means that inside the central parts of certain tiny lobes within the liver, cells have been killed off by the action of hostile enzymes. Again, not an uncommon finding, but in combination with a yellowish or tan liver, it indicates something other than alcoholic poisoning. As a toxicologist, I knew these were signs found in fatal poisoning with high concentrations of paracetamol."

No checks for the presence of legal drugs had been made on any of the bodies, so there was no recorded proof that pharmaceutical substances had been present in the girls' systems.

"However, I was convinced this was criminal territory," Perlosio said. "The more I thought about it, and the more I read and re-read the autopsy reports, the more it seemed to me that I was examining superficial evidence of large-scale deliberate poisoning."

Perlosio was so sure of his ground that he took on the massive job of applying for exhumations of the nine women who had been buried. Two bodies, to his annoyance, had been cremated.

Families resisted and so did the Catholic Church. Even in present-day Spain, an exhumation is considered to be a shocking violation of decency. In pressing his case, Perlosio assured those who opposed him that he intended to disrupt the peace of the dead only in the greater interests of serving justice.

"It is uncanny how a light disturbance of the moral tradition can produce explosive effects," said Miguel Barea, a freelance journalist based in Barcelona. Barea followed the case at the prompting of his wife, an English social historian, who saw the dramatic potential of the story. "Because Jorge Perlosio followed his professional curiosity along a natural path, which involved ruffling a taboo, he was almost killed."

Eleven days after the first applications for exhumation had been made, Perlosio visited a cemetery where one of the young women from his case study was buried. The purpose of his visit was to obtain samples of earth: he would collect similar samples from all the burial sites, so that irrelevant soil traces found in the decomposed remains could be eliminated whenever they were detected, thus saving valuable time and resources.

"So there I was," Perlosio said, "squatting by a grave with my trowel and my paper cup. Suddenly I was seized from behind, dragged to my feet and shoved up against a tree. My attacker was a priest, a young one, and he was powerfully built. He was also very angry; in fact he looked deranged. He held me against the tree with both hands pressed on my shoulders, and when he shouted at me he showered my face with spit."

The priest had heard that Perlosio wanted a body exhumed from the local cemetery. The news had incensed him and he had preached a sermon against the "encroachment of godless elements intent on visiting blasphemy against the interred flesh of the sacred dead."

"When he learned I was actually to visit the cemetery in person," Perlosio said, "he got there ahead of me and lurked among the trees, waiting. He had brought a knife with him, a big kitchen knife with a sharp serrated blade, and he yelled right in my face that he was going to plunge it into my heart. According to some moral code he failed to specify, this was the required treatment for blasphemers like myself."

The priest did in fact try to stab Perlosio, but the point of the knife was nowhere nearly as sharp as the edge and it didn't even penetrate his coat. When that failed the priest began slashing about wildly with the knife, cutting Perlosio's face, neck and hands, and severing a vein in the priest's own wrist. By that time someone had called the police and the priest was dragged away.

"After mountainous paperwork, weeks of haggling and wrangling, and that astounding act of violence against me," Perlosio said, "I was able to get exhumation orders in seven cases."

Arrangements were made to have the exhumations performed at dead of night, on dates which were not made public. In spite of that, spectators did show up at five of the sites and several even took souvenir photographs of the coffins being pulled out of the earth.

Three of the bodies had been reduced to a slime of chemicals and loose bones in the bottoms of the coffins; one had turned to a rubbery substance called adipocere; two were little more than dried skeletons; the seventh, having been dead only three months and buried in a cemetery in the snowy Deborio mountains, was relatively fresh.

"Getting usable tissue samples from six decayed corpses was not easy," Perlosio said. "However, in the end we gathered enough to produce a respectable record of each girl's chemistry at the time of her death."

Advanced chromatography was used to perform analysis on bone, ligament, liver, muscle-fibre and traces of abdominal tissue, including bowel and stomach fragments. Chromatography, at its most basic, is a method of separating two or more chemical compounds in solution—either by passing the solution down a column of powdered absorbent, or across the surface of absorbent paper—during which process the various components of the solution adhere to the absorbent material at different points, according to their chemical characteristics, by which they can be identified.

As soon as tissue types were determined, they were, in Perlosio's words, "analysed to annihilation." High concentrations of paracetamol were found in the tissues of all seven bodies. "I gauged the average concentration to be about 250 milligrams per litre of blood. That's enough to kill anyone. The presence of alcohol, which of course was determined in every case, would have aggravated the poisonous action."

So, over a period of twenty-five months, at least seven young women in the region of the Costa del Sol had died from the combined toxic effects of concentrated paracetamol and alcohol. Furthermore, there was enough consistency in the sampling to suggest that the alcohol present, in every case, was the same brand of bottled beer. These findings were too much for coincidence.

"I had been sure before," Perlosio said, "but now I was on fire with certainty. The cumulative effect of opposition and extremely difficult investigative work was a kind of avid euphoria—I was overjoyed that my suspicions were being so outstandingly vindicated, and I was desperately restless to follow our conclusions wherever they might lead. Since I am at heart a detective, I wanted above everything else to catch the person or persons who had killed these girls."

The analysis of the beer was carried out by Perlosio's assistant, Juan Lafadio, who admitted that the early stages of his analysis were far from scientific.

"The body that had been buried in icy ground began to decay quickly once we had it in our mortuary," he said. "The effects of various liberated amino acids intensify the aromas given off by the process of decay, and when I examined the liver I was sure I recognised a particular beer smell. I asked one of the mortuary attendants and he recognised it too. We de-

cided it was *Aguijón*, a strong bottled beer made by
a commercial brewery at Mijas."

Lafadio made a chemical sampling from the alcohol in the dead girl's liver and it was eventually confirmed to be *Aguijón*. Comparative tests on the other
bodies confirmed that major alcohol traces present in
their tissues were of the same potent beer.

"This was a tidy refinement of our investigation,"
Perlosio said, "but it didn't take us any closer to sug-
gesting a line of enquiry for the police. There are
many, many bars on the Costa del Sol, and nearly all
of them sell *Aguijón*. However, following the first
analysis our senior chemist sent me a memo. It said
that the chemical breakdown of the beer, as I had
submitted it, was certainly a match for *Aguijón*, but
they now noticed it had an extra ingredient, perhaps
some kind of oil. The same finding applied to all
seven samples. We had *Aguijón* plus something else—
but what?"

Juan Lafadio was set the task of trawling the bars
on the Costa del Sol, aided by a team of volunteer
laboratory technicians and assistants, with a view to
finding out what substances barmen added to the beer
they sold. Over a three-week period they bought several hundred bottles of *Aguijón* with various substances added: "Everything from brown sugar to
fermented date juice. The guys actually prised off the
tops of the bottles, put in their own flavour enhance-
ment, and recapped them. The added ingredients were
supposed to be secret, of course, but they were dead
easy to identify."

One bottle out of the hundreds tested displayed the same chemical characteristics as the samples taken from the dead girls. A thorough analysis was made and careful comparisons conducted between the fresh beer samples and the polluted ones taken from the dead girls. The added substance was finally pigeon-holed as myristica, commonly known as nutmeg.

"The bar owner who sold it to our researchers couldn't say where the bottle had come from. There were no others in his bar, so he assumed it was one he had bought somewhere himself on a day off, hadn't got around to drinking it, and had simply added it to his stock."

A profound gloom settled on Perlosio's team. They had hit a dead end, but the despondency didn't last long.

"The information about the specially doctored *Aguijón* rang a bell in an interesting quarter," said Perlosio. "Two detectives who spent the summer months monitoring the drug trade along the Costa knew a bar where one of the specialities was *Aguijón* with a dash of nutmeg. There was some secret to the way it was done, because the nutmeg did not interfere with the gas in the beer, as it would if it were simply stirred in."

The police visited the bar, which was in Solabreña, and learned that although the nutmeg speciality had originated there, it had now been taken up by four other bar owners, in four different towns, who had paid a fee to retain local exclusivity, and to learn the secret of adding the nutmeg without interfering with the usual properties of *Aguijón*.

"Staff at the bar in Solabreña did not recognize any of the girls in the pictures we showed them," a senior detective said. "Police visited the four other bars where the speciality was being sold—in Fuengirola, Marbella, Estepona and Casares—and in one of them, *La Pandereta* in Casares, a waiter said he had seen two of the girls and possibly a third at different times. After thinking it over for a while, he told the detectives he was sure that each of the girls had been in the bar with a character known as Doc."

Doc was the nickname of a male nurse from a local private hospital. He haunted the bar at weekends.

"As soon as the waiter started to describe Doc, we knew we were on to something," the senior detective said. "This man was habitually depressed, he was forever starting arguments, and he had a rabid dislike of Englishmen and Germans, especially those who successfully picked up Spanish girls. 'People should stick to their own kind,' was a slogan he shouted when he was drunk."

The detectives were told tales of Doc attacking men he suspected of "defiling" Spanish girls, and he had once slashed the tyres on a hired car parked in the forecourt of the bar, because the Englishman renting the car had turned up with a Spanish-looking woman—who turned out to be his German wife.

"A lot of Doc's trouble came from the fact that he was physically ugly," the senior detective said. "He had a nasty compulsive personality, too, and he desperately wanted to pick up girls, Spanish girls. They would usually have nothing to do with him, because he was such a fright, and he obviously had no money."

Doc, whose real name was Federico Bascos, denied ever knowing the girls in the pictures. He also threatened to make a case of the harassment which he felt was being inflicted on him. He resisted every attempt at rational interview, and in the end he threw such tantrums, and hurled such foul and noisy abuse, that the police felt it best to leave him alone, even though they were sure, by now, that he was implicated in multiple murder.

"To try to strengthen the case against Federico Bascos, we carried out one final chemical analysis," Perlosio said. "Frankly, I couldn't believe such a long shot would pay off. What we did, specifically, was attempt to ascribe a manufacturing identity to the paracetamol in the dead girls' bodies. Miracle of miracles, we did it."

The paracetamol had an identifying characteristic which narrowed it down to one therapeutic product from one company, which happened to be a small pharmaceutical manufacturer at La Linea, near Casares. Enquiries at the firm established that Federico Bascos made regular visits there, ostensibly on behalf of his employers, to purchase their special paracetamol linctus which contained an extra pain-killer—dextropropoxyphene—which was present in the compound the dead girls had taken.

Bascos was interviewed again and confronted with the weight of evidence against him.

"His defence of himself," said the senior detective, "was a masterpiece of advanced paranoia."

Bascos ranted and shouted; he shut himself in a bottle store in the bar and shouted at the detectives through the open transom.

"He told us he was perfectly aware of what we were doing, and that we would not succeed. He knew that, because of his special insights, he was regarded as a threat to law enforcement, which was geared to controlling the ordinary people and eliminating free-thinkers like himself."

Efforts were made to cajole Bascos and make him leave the cupboard, but instead of coming out he stood on an up-ended beer crate and started waving his fists at the police.

"He swore he would bring down the administration that made a policy of persecuting him like this," the senior detective said, "and he would, furthermore, pursue each and every policeman involved in the attempt to overthrow his standing as a human being— a *special* human being who chose to live within a society desperately in need of men with his instinct and clarity of vision.

"What we did, finally," the detective said, "was just let him burn his anger out."

In the end Bascos left the little room, and two hours later he buckled under questioning.

"The irony in this case," said the senior detective, "was that Bascos had no idea he'd been committing murder. He was nothing but a fool, a clown with a dream of power. He had no killer's impulses."

Perlosio agreed. Bascos, he said, was a simple-minded victim of delusion. "He had plied these female transients with beer laced with paracetamol linctus, a combination which he seriously believed would relax their inhibitions and inflame their sexuality. What it did was make them drowsy, so he had a few successes, because some girls were too sleepy to stop him doing what he wanted to do."

Believing in the sexually stimulating properties of the spiced beer, and being certain that paracetamol erased inhibitions, Bascos had created what he believed was a powerful aphrodisiac cocktail.

"He added so much of the linctus that it became a lethal mixture," said Perlosio. "But in spite of that, it couldn't kill anyone there and then. Even in massive overdose there is never a rapid death from paracetamol poisoning. Death is delayed for two to four days as liver failure develops. Two to four days after swallowing a couple of pints of Doc's toxic cocktail, these highly mobile young women were miles away, with nothing to connect them to that bar in Casares."

Early in 1994 Federico Bascos was charged on seven counts of homicide. The case never went to court, because Bascos was found to be unfit to plead. Three psychiatrists independently certified that he was suffering from advanced delusional schizophrenia, so a trial was out of the question. Instead, he was committed for an indeterminate period to a secure psychiatric hospital.

Six months after being committed, Bascos asked to speak to a priest. He reported that he had been visited in his room by a messenger of Saint Camillus, the patron saint of nurses, who had commanded that he tell a priest how many girls had taken his poisonous mixture. He had thought hard and carefully, and he believed that over a period of two-and-a-half years, the figure was thirty-one, although it could have been thirty-two.

"We can only assume," said Jorge Perlosio, "that of the numerous young women who died on the Costa del Sol between 1991 and early 1993, a good number would still be alive if they had not met Federico Bascos."

FOUR

VENDETTA

In the city of Glasgow in 1957 the youth movement was having a slow start. The trends and fashions that would explode into the revolution of the sixties could scarcely get a foothold, mainly because the restrictive licensing hours in Glasgow—and throughout Scotland—meant that no one could buy an alcoholic drink at a public place after nine o'clock in the evening. On a Saturday night, things went quiet in Glasgow at approximately the time they were beginning to get lively south of the border.

There were answers to the problem. People would buy "carry-outs" of beer and spirits and use them as entrée to parties. No one was a gate-crasher if he brought plenty of drink with him. That, however, was not the same as going out for the night. Ending up in someone's smoky, overcrowded tenement flat did nothing to engender a sense of fun and freedom.

"It was a desperate situation, when you look back on it," said David Turnbull, a detective inspector with the City of Glasgow police during the 1960s. "People struggled to have a good time within a system that was definitely designed to hamper them. The Saturday-night tenement parties were all very well, but that wasn't what people needed—they wanted to go on the town, they wanted to mingle on truly common ground. The brutal licensing laws made sure that wouldn't happen."

An ironical offshoot of the restrictions was that the streets of Glasgow could be dangerous at night, and the main danger came from drunks. Even partial prohibition produces an ugly backlash. People would go into pubs in the evening knowing that they had only a couple of hours before the grilles came down and they were thrown out. So they drank at a furious rate, consuming as much in an hour as a person in Birmingham or London might drink in two hours, or three.

"I've seen them blind drunk and walking into lamp posts," Turnbull said. "I've stood and watched two men trying to have a fight and being so drunk they couldn't even hit each other. Drunks can be hilarious, but when they're all over the place they're a menace. From my own experience in Glasgow I know of drunk men who have caused tragedies, then wakened up the next day and not remembered anything."

Billy Semple was 18 in 1957. He was a pharmacy

student at Glasgow University, and three nights a week he worked as a junior barman at one of the oldest pubs in Glasgow, on York Street, near the famous Broomielaw. Junior barmen in those days did most of the menial work, like washing glasses, cleaning out slop trays, waiting on tables and emptying ashtrays. The arrangement suited Billy. The work was steady and undemanding, it paid enough to cover the rent for his one-room flat on Great Western Road, with a little left over, and while he was slaving away in the scruffy old pub he wasn't spending anything. Billy's girlfriend, Laura Bennett, was also a pharmacy student. They planned to marry when they were both qualified and settled in secure positions. On the nights Billy worked in the pub Laura had a job in the box office of a cinema on Sauchiehall Street.

"They were a nice, decent couple," said Turnbull. "They were responsible and forward looking. It did my heart good to meet people like that—bright, civilised young folk with a view of their future and the will to make it happen. Then, one night they turned a corner at the wrong time and their future got cancelled by a bunch of thugs."

It happened on Clyde Street, near St. Andrew's Roman Catholic Church. The couple had been with friends at a pub on Jamaica Street, and at closing time they walked down towards the river, where Billy planned to see Laura on to the bus that would take her home to Uddingston.

"A woman at a bus stop across the street saw them turn the corner on to Clyde Street," Turnbull said, "and she remembered wishing they hadn't, because at that moment three men in their twenties, obviously drunk, were walking towards the corner of Jamaica Street. From the way they shouted and kept looking around them as they walked, they were clearly on the lookout for trouble."

The men saw Billy and Laura and immediately spread out, standing shoulder to shoulder, blocking the pavement. Billy took Laura by the elbow and stepped on to the road to go past. The man nearest the road reached out and pulled Laura's hair as she hurried past. She cried out and the man turned, getting hold of her hair with both hands, pulling hard and dragging her on to her back in the gutter. His friends cheered him on and when Billy tried to help Laura, one of them hit him in the face with a bottle.

"The witness saw Billy drop to his knees and she heard the horrible clunk when the thug hit him with the bottle again. He hit Billy with it a third time, right on top of the head, and it came down so hard it broke. Billy fell down and they lost interest in him. The three of them then dragged and half-carried Laura to the corner, held her there until a bus came roaring along the cobbles, then threw her in front of it."

Billy was found to be dead on arrival at the Royal Infirmary. Laura died in the same place an hour later, from multiple injuries.

"I was in charge of the investigation," Turnbull said. "It was a disheartening job with next to nothing to go on. The female witness could provide a detailed account of everything that happened, but she had no idea what the assailants looked like. She said she had been so frightened just being there, and so scared for the young couple, that she kept looking at them and hoping they would get away. The impression she had of the three attackers was one I'd heard before, many times—loud, behaving wildly, using foul language. Nothing of their appearance had stuck with her. The bus driver didn't see them, either. He had been ploughing along Clyde Street the way he had for years, and all of a sudden there was this girl flying into his headlights, and he braked and felt the nearside front wheel go over her. He was too shocked to see where the thugs went or what they looked like."

At Billy's funeral Turnbull was approached by a tall man in a black suit. He had the fastidious bearing of a lawyer, Turnbull thought. The man was in fact a doctor, Angus Semple, a pathologist with the Medical Examiner's Department of the Chicago Police Authority. He was also Billy Semple's brother.

"He introduced himself and asked me if there had been any progress in finding the people who killed Billy and Laura. I told him the truth, which was that we had one witness, who was of no use in making an identification, and that was it. No other avenues of investigation had presented themselves, although we were still making enquiries."

Dr. Semple then astonished Turnbull by telling him that in the four days since his arrival in Glasgow from the United States, he had conducted an informal investigation of his own, and he believed he knew the identity of one of the men involved in the double murder.

"For three nights I stood on that stretch of Clyde Street where it happened," Semple told Turnbull, "and when anyone came past, I asked them politely if they could help. I asked them if they had perhaps passed that way the previous week, and if they had, did they see three young men behaving in a disorderly fashion. I must have questioned a hundred people over the three-night period. The one clue I got came from an old man, on the second night."

The man was lame and leaned heavily on a stick. He told Semple that he had seen the three young men and had given them a wide berth, a manoeuvre he had perfected over the years. He had recognised one of the three—Tommy Lyle's oldest boy, he said. He believed the name was Eric, and he warned Dr. Semple that this was not a young man to tangle with.

"Tommy Lyle was an illegal off-track bookmaker," Turnbull said. "He was well known to the police, and to workmen along the Broomielaw and the Anderston Quay who placed bets with him. Dr. Semple found out where Tommy lived, and a little further enquiry revealed that his son Eric lived there too. I said I hoped Dr. Semple hadn't approached Eric Lyle. No, he said, that was my job, now he'd got the investigation moving for me."

Turnbull checked the records and found that Eric Lyle had been fined four times for assault and jailed once for causing grievous bodily harm to a female shopkeeper. He had also been charged on two occasions with attempted rape, but neither charge had held up. Turnbull made circumspect enquiries around Eric Lyle's known haunts and learned that he had two friends who were usually with him when he went out drinking—they were Ben Craig and Steve Duncan.

"I checked the records again," Turnbull said. "Both men were well represented. Craig had fines and sentences for assault and theft, Duncan had done two years in Barlinnie for aggravated burglary."

Eric Lyle, Ben Craig and Steve Duncan were picked up and brought to Central Police Headquarters. Turnbull questioned Lyle, while two other officers grilled Craig and Duncan. All three detectives had long experience of interrogation and knew the range of tricks and tactics. They knew how to make one suspect nervous about what another might be saying. Even so, they found that Lyle and his pals were ready for them.

"After two hours we gave up," Turnbull said. "I tried everything, so did my colleagues. We knew now they were guilty, because only three guilty men would have got their story so tightly tailored and stitched. They all told the same tale, none of them said anything to contradict either of the other two. From an interrogation standpoint, they were unassailable. We had to let them go."

Dr. Semple called on Turnbull the day after the three men had been questioned. Turnbull told him what had happened. Semple was not impressed. He asked why there had been no search of the men's homes, no forensic examination of their clothing.

"I was finding it hard to be polite to this man," Turnbull said. "He was obviously very bright, he was aggressive in a positive way, and I could only admire his determination to get something solid on Lyle, Craig and Duncan. The irritating part was his obvious assumption that I couldn't be trusted to do my job without somebody like him supervising me. He had scored impressively, I would never deny that, but that didn't give him the right to push me around."

Turnbull held on to his temper. He told Dr. Semple that so much time had elapsed since the murders that any search of the suspects' homes, forensic or otherwise, would inevitably be fruitless. Semple obviously didn't agree with that, but he didn't take the matter of a search any further.

"Let me make my purpose clear, Inspector," he said. "Being realistic, I don't foresee that we could ever bring a cast-iron case against these men for murder. I'm not harbouring a forlorn hope that they'll be brought before a judge, that is no part of my purpose. What I need—*all* I need—is to know for sure that they are the ones who killed my brother and his girlfriend."

Turnbull relented slightly and told Semple that if it was any help, he was sure the three men were the ones who committed the murders. They were certainly together on that night, witnesses in two city-centre pubs had seen them, and when they were questioned they didn't deny they had been together.

"So I told Dr. Semple, if one of them was guilty, they all were, and from my questioning of the smug, alibi-perfect Eric Lyle, I had no doubt he was guilty."

Semple thanked Turnbull. He said he didn't doubt the instinct that told the detectives that Lyle, Craig and Duncan were guilty, but for himself he needed a minimum of one piece of hard evidence before he would let himself be sure.

At that point, Turnbull said, it never occurred to him to wonder why Semple so badly needed to be sure. "If I did think anything about it, I suppose I thought he was like any other sideline casualty of a crime, he wanted certainty rather than doubt, even if he could do nothing about it."

Before Semple left the office that day, he asked Turnbull if any concrete evidence at all had been found. Only the broken bottle, Turnbull said. Semple looked startled. Did Turnbull mean the bottle that had been used to club Billy Semple to death?

"That's right," Turnbull told him. "It's in smithereens, though, and the fragments lay in the road for an hour or more before they were gathered up. Our people say they have no investigative significance."

Semple said he would like to examine the pieces nevertheless. Turnbull called his superiors and told them. By then, the reputation of Dr. Semple had spread around headquarters. It had been intensified by an article about him that somebody found in an American magazine, where he was described as the Spilsbury of Chicago—a reference to Sir Bernard Spilsbury, at one time the most influential pathologist in the UK and much admired in America.

"The powers said Dr. Semple could certainly ex-

amine the bottle fragments—they even added that if
he needed any technical facilities, he was free to use
the small laboratory at the city mortuary on the Salt-
market."

Semple took them up on the offer.

Less than a week after he had borrowed the bottle
fragments, he returned them to police headquarters,
loose in a box as he had received them. He thanked
Turnbull for his help, and Turnbull asked just how
much help the bits of bottle had been.

"Well, these things always help in the process of
elimination," Semple replied. Turnbull realised he had
been told nothing. He was about to put his question
another way when Semple said he would like to ask
one final favour. "I would like to study the criminal
records of Lyle, Craig and Duncan."

Again, Turnbull's superiors had no hesitation in
granting the request. He took the papers away and
promised he would return them in the morning.

"He brought them back just as he had promised,"
Turnbull said. "He thanked me again for everything,
and donated six bottles of whisky to the department
as a thank-you for our co-operation. As far as we were
concerned, that was that."

Three days later, a body fished out of the River
Clyde at the Kingston Bridge was identified as that of
Ben Craig, one of the three men suspected of mur-
dering Billy Semple and Laura Bennett.

"As soon as I heard, I was over at the mortuary
like a shot," Turnbull said. "It was definitely Craig
and he was definitely dead, and as far as the pathol-

ogist could tell, he had died of drowning. There were no marks of violence on the body. It was to all appearances an accidental death."

Turnbull was aware that Dr. Semple was still in Glasgow—on his last visit to headquarters he had mentioned he was extending his visit in order to help with the rehabilitation of his mother, who had been desolated by the death of Billy.

"I decided I'd call and tell him what had happened to Craig. He took the news calmly. 'It was only justice,' he said, and thanked me for calling."

Three days after Craig was fished out of the river, Steve Duncan, one of the other two suspects, was found lying in an alley near Glasgow Cross. He was dead. Again, there were no marks of violence on the body. The Procurator Fiscal ordered an autopsy and it was found that Duncan had died of alcohol poisoning.

"The level of ethanol in his blood," the pathologist told Turnbull, "would have been enough to despatch two men."

In Duncan's stomach alone was a quantity of cheap brandy equivalent to a half-litre bottle. The only conclusion to be drawn was that he drank and drank until he passed out from hyper-intoxication.

"I was now feeling very uneasy," Turnbull said. "I called Dr. Semple and asked if we could meet. He suggested the bar at the Central hotel. When I saw him I came straight to the point. The deaths of Craig and Duncan were too much for coincidence, I said. He agreed with me. So I asked him right out, did he know anything about those deaths? He smiled, and I have to say it was disarming. I apologised straight away. I think about it now and I cringe, but it happened, I didn't even make him defend himself. I apologised before he had a chance to say anything."

The two men had a drink, and Turnbull talked about how hard it was to see a pattern when most of the time the facts were unknown. Semple said that was the story of his life back in Chicago. All we can do, he told Turnbull, is keep looking for the truth, and try, always, to keep from presuming too much.

"Two days after we had that drink, the remaining suspect, Eric Lyle, was found dead in a walk-in freezer at the wholesale butcher's where he worked. As far as anyone could tell, he had walked into the freezer without putting the door-block in place, which in those days was the only safety measure adopted by many owners of industrial freezers. There were no marks of violence on the body.

"So all three were dead. I felt sick. I was sure now that Semple must have bumped them off, but there was no case to pursue—these men had all died accidentally—on the face of it, nothing was clearer."

For his own satisfaction, Turnbull went to the mortuary and asked the senior attendant if he had any idea what Dr. Semple was doing during the time he was working in the little laboratory there. The attendant was cagey at first, until Turnbull promised him that whatever he said, it would not be used against him in any way. In that case, the attendant said, he was happy to admit that, out of sheer curiosity, he had spied on Dr. Semple.

Semple had shown the attendant the fragments of bottle and asked him to identify the type of bottle from the shape and size of its neck. The attendant told him it was a large Tennent's Pale Ale bottle, of the type known as a screwtop. Semple then asked the attendant to get him an unbroken one exactly like it.

The next day, when Semple called at the mortuary, the attendant gave him the bottle he had asked for. "He said he would like to be left alone, so I left him, but I watched what he was doing through a gap in the partition between the lab and the office. It was fascinating, even though for a while I'd no idea what he was up to."

Semple made a mixture of plaster of Paris and poured it into the empty bottle, filling it to the top. He pushed a piece of dowel rod into the neck and held it there until the plaster began to harden around it. He then set the bottle aside and left the laboratory, locking the door and pocketing the key. He told the attendant he would be back in a few hours.

When he returned and locked himself into the lab again, the attendant got back to his peephole. Semple examined the bottle. The plaster had set hard. Using the dowel protruding from the neck of the bottle as a handle, he took a small hammer and gently tapped the side of the bottle until it cracked. He did that several more times, crazing the whole surface of the glass. Then he held it over a waste bin and gave the bottle three sharp taps with the hammer. The glass fell away in dozens of shards, leaving behind a plaster replica of the bottle.

The attendant said that was when the work really happened. Semple spread sheets of clean shelf paper across the bench and turned on a strong overhead lamp. He then put on latex gloves and opened the box in which the police had placed the collected fragments of the bottle they picked up in Clyde Street. One by one he removed the fragments and placed them on the paper covering the bench.

"It took me a while to catch on," the attendant said. "He would pick up a bit of glass, hold it against the side of the plaster replica, then he'd put it down again and try other bits. Then, when he began sticking the bits of glass in place with paper paste, I got it. He was rebuilding the broken bottle, putting it together like a jigsaw puzzle round the plaster shape.

"When he stopped working that night he had built maybe a quarter. He threw a cloth over it and another cloth over the loose pieces of glass, then he locked the lab door and said he would be back in the morning."

It took Semple three days to complete the reconstruction of the bottle. When it was finished, he sat looking at it for a long time.

"There were hardly any bits missing," the attendant said, "only tiny slivers here and there. If you looked at it casually, you were looking at a whole bottle. He'd done a brilliant job. Then he dusted it all over with powder from a rubber puffer bulb. That took him a long time. When it was done, he went over the surface with a camel brush, careful as anything."

The attendant realised he had been too long at the spyhole and he went back to his duties. As he worked, he was aware of a flashgun firing in the laboratory, and as he passed he smelled the familiar odour of burnt shellac given off by spent flashbulbs.

"It dawned on me like the rush of a hangover," Turnbull said. "He must have got a print on the bottle, and photographed it. Then he borrowed the records so he could find out if the print belonged to any of the three suspects. And I'll bet it did.

"But Semple didn't want us to act on the finding of that print, even though it would have been a powerful weapon in the hands of the prosecution. He dismantled the bottle and cleaned the pieces before he gave it back to us. I tried to call him again, not sure what I was going to say this time, but he had already gone back to Chicago. There was no use chasing him, either. There wasn't any case to answer."

It seemed more than likely that Semple had solved the case, but he did not want conventional justice. Later, Turnbull remembered what he had said back at the start: "What I need—*all* I need—is to know for sure that they are the ones who killed my brother and his girlfriend."

David Turnbull, and a few others, have remained convinced that Dr. Angus Semple murdered Ben Craig, Steve Duncan and Eric Lyle.

"If it's true, and no one could convince me it's not, then it was a hell of a trick," Turnbull said. "He solved a case that we couldn't even get started on, then he wiped out the perpetrators without leaving one mark or sign that could incriminate him."

It had never been his practice to admire or lionise criminals, Turnbull added, but if he ever had to make an exception, he knew who it would be.

FIVE

PENFRIEND

The city of Bergamo is situated in Lombardy in northern Italy, twenty kilometres south-east of Lake Como. Originally the centre of the Orobi tribe, it became the Roman town of Bergomom in 196 BC. Some years later it had to be rebuilt after being destroyed by Attila the Hun. Later still, it was the scat of the Lombard duchy and in the twelfth century became an independent settlement. After 1329 it was ruled by the Milanese Visconti family, then in 1428 it passed to Venice. In 1729 the French took control of Bergamo and made it a part of the Cisalpine Republic, which was established by Napoleon. In 1815 it became Austrian, then in 1859 it was absorbed into the Italian kingdom.

"Our history is spectacular and colourful," said Dr.

Domenico Fortini, a retired forensic chemist. "Today, Bergamo is as fine a place, materially, as it ever was. In the upper town, the older part, we have the cathedral, and the beautiful Cappella Colleoni with ceiling frescoes painted by Tiepolo. Then there's the Rocca, which is a magnificent fourteenth-century castle that houses two superb museums. The composer Donizetti was born here and his birthplace is perfectly preserved. I could go on and on. I came here at the age of ten and I have lived in the same house since. Bergamo beguiles me, I am enchanted by the place even to this day."

However, there have been times, Fortini admits, when his feelings for the city have been uncomfortably mixed. "Apart from being historically and culturally significant, Bergamo is also an industrial centre. There are textile mills; engineering works; cement, mechanical and electrical manufacturers. Industry has always brought prosperity, I am sure, but it also brings greed, and greed is the thin edge of crime. Some of the crimes I've had to involve myself with, they make me realise that the noble streak in mankind is very slender, and it is easily obliterated."

In 1966, the population of Bergamo was 122,000. Today it is roughly 5,000 less than that. Industry in the region boomed in the sixties and the local crime rate had never been higher. Fortini, recently qualified, was employed by the government to supplement a regional forensic team based in an office complex at Modena, a few kilometres north-east of Bergamo.

"They took themselves very seriously," said Luciano Lattes, a former police detective with *Polizia Centrale* in Bergamo. "I used to hate going out there, waiting about in that smelly little lab of theirs while some snotty kid in a white coat gave me his verdict on whatever specimens they had been testing for us. Dr. Fortini was OK, though. He took himself seriously, too, but he had good reason. He was hot stuff, even back then."

Fortini had distinguished himself in his third month with the forensic team. A case of sudden death in a young female athlete had baffled pathologists, who had made two thorough autopsy examinations of the body without finding a hint of any disorder or weakness that could have accounted for the death. There were no signs of violence on the body, no evidence of a struggle of any kind. Foul play had been ruled out, but the death was still a complete mystery.

Fortini read the police and medical findings, and he was curious to know why the body had been lying on the living room carpet with both arms outstretched above the head.

"I had never heard of a body being found like that," he said. "When I said so to the officers in charge of the case they looked at me as if I was just a silly boy, which in their view I probably was. But it did strike me as terribly odd, even though everyone else seemed to accept it was just one of those things—a person dies suddenly, the body flops down and the arms end up stretched above the head. I was sure there had to be a stronger reason than that, and I was furthermore convinced that the reason was linked to the cause of death."

Fortini was given permission to examine the place where the woman died. It was a one-room apartment in the lower town, a poorly maintained place with damp on the walls and ceiling and a pervasive odour of mildew.

"I was surprised anyone with athletic tendencies would stay in such a place," he said. "But the police pointed out that the dead girl had worked in a factory and her pay was very small. She was considered lucky to have a place of her own at all, since most girls her age were forced to stay at home, usually in over-crowded conditions, and help support the family. So what I was looking at was the home of an independent Italian female, *circa* 1966. It was pretty sad."

The police had marked the place on the carpet where the body was found. Fortini stood beside the chalked outline, trying to imagine the scene moments before the girl died. His comments are curiously similar to those of forensic officer Jack Dexter, quoted in a previous chapter, when he tried to empathise with the time of a death by immersing himself in the atmosphere of the place where it happened.

"Some professionals have said it's a valid technique, standing there in the actual place where it happened, surrounded by the sights and smells, giving myself access to every scrap of aura that might re-create the event, or events, that caused the young woman to die. But no, it did no good at all. All I could imagine was her dropping dead suddenly, with her hands above her head."

That proved to be the triggering thought. The image Fortini had in his head at that moment was of the girl holding her hands above her head a moment *before* she died.

"It was an uncalculated thought," he said. "It just came. So I stood roughly where she must have stood and I stretched my arms above my head. I felt a tickle on my knuckles and looked up. I was touching the fringes of the lampshade."

He strode across the room and turned on the light switch by the door. The light flickered, came on for a couple of seconds, then went out again.

"I was sure I knew what had happened," Fortini said. "The correct procedure would have been for me to go back to the lab and collect electrical testing equipment, but I was too excited, too young, to be frank. I had no patience. I stood under the lamp, just where the girl would have stood, and I reached up to the light bulb. I tapped it and nothing happened. So I stood on my toes and tapped a little higher. Still nothing. I reached up to the place where the metal lampshade support was connected to the light fitting, and as I touched it I received a violent electric shock."

Fortini was stunned for a moment. When he regained his senses he found he was sitting on the carpet, inside the chalk outline of the corpse.

"I left the apartment, had a coffee to steady myself, then went straight to the police mortuary. A pathologist with a condescending manner agreed to let me look at the girl's body. I examined the fingertips and found a tiny blister under the rim of the nail on the right forefinger. Then I examined the feet. On the left heel there was another blister, not much larger than the one on her finger."

The pathologist soon changed his approach when he realised what Fortini had discovered.

"There was no doubt about it, she had been electrocuted. The light had probably failed on her, just as it had on me, and when she touched the metal cross-strut on the lamp-shape she received enough of a jolt to kill her. She was barefoot when they found her, which means she made a perfect contact with the damp carpet. The current would have passed through her like water down a pipe."

A call was made to a specialist in physiology in Rome, and he confirmed that the findings in cases of electrocution are often so insignificant that only the most careful searching will find them. He added that entry and exit blistering were frequently the only signs.

"So, in 1966, when we had a spate of really strange murders to deal with," Detective Lattes said, "one of my superiors suggested we sound out young Dr. Fortini and get his thinking on the mystery."

Up to that point, Fortini knew nothing about the cases. For several weeks he had been engaged on a complex series of analyses on blood specimens related to a disputed insurance claim, and that had absorbed his time and attention to the exclusion of everything else.

"Even to the exclusion of my wife, who left me at approximately that time," Fortini said. "Three years we had been married, that was all. It was long enough for her. She said it was worse than being married to a policeman. At least when a cop got home late, as usual, he didn't stink like a chemical factory, and he didn't take his notes to bed with him."

The series of murders presented Fortini with a welcome diversion. "What was intriguing," he said, "was that it took the police eight weeks to realise it *was* a series. These were not stupid men on the case, remember. They were all experienced homicide detectives. They were simply confronted with the facts in such a random, wide-spaced order, and with so much confusing and distracting intermediate matter, that a linking thread was not apparent."

There were four murders, all men, and the first link observed by the police was that all four had been released from prison a few days before they were killed.

"What slowed up the identification of a link," said Detective Lattes, "was that the four men had been released from different prisons, at different dates, over a period of seven months. Three of them were on the books as unsolved homicides when the fourth was murdered in Bergamo. That was when the officer collating statistics at *Polizia Centrale* noticed the link. If we'd had a computer in the station in those days, it would have spotted a potential trend by the time murder number two was on record."

The second link, which was noticed shortly after the first, was that all four murder victims were sex offenders. Victims A and B had been sentenced for committing rape on minors, victim C was described on his record as a habitual molester of young women, and victim D was jailed after a charge of sexual murder had been commuted, due to inadequately prepared prosecution evidence, to manslaughter.

"They all died pretty horribly," Lattes said. "A, B and C were castrated, apparently with a razor, and left to bleed to death. Victim D was castrated then shot in the knees, probably to stop him running. He bled to death, too."

The fourth murder was committed behind a factory building in Bergamo lower town; the other three happened in towns nearby—Lecco, Rovota and Brescia.

"For the sake of centralising the investigation," Lattes said, "it was decided that the series be investigated, in the light of the newly discovered linking factors, by the Bergamo police. One week into the investigation we realised we were up against a brick wall. There were no leads. The trails on all four cases were cold, if they had ever existed in the first place. The tiny pieces of new evidence we gathered on the dead men added nothing but confusion to the investigation.

"That was when Dr. Fortini was approached. Apart from the electrocution case, he had shown himself astute in later investigations, too. He had a nose for detective work, and he was also a very diplomatic person. The detectives felt he was the man most likely to get us out of our predicament without creating any disturbance, and without crowing about his success afterwards."

Upon examining the records of the dead men, Fortini discovered yet another linking factor. All four had been given comparatively light sentences for their crimes. Further checking in newspaper files showed that the forbearing sentences had all been cited in news stories during 1964, the year when the men were jailed. The stories repeatedly highlighted a "cult of leniency" that was sweeping through Italy's criminal court system.

"I was soon halfway convinced that the murders had been triggered by media reports of those four cases, which were cited over and over again as evidence of our judiciary's slackening grip on the notion of punishment."

Pressure from the press and the public eventually brought a response from Italy's President, Giuseppe Saragat, and premier Aldo Moro, who in 1965 jointly announced that a programme of "re-education in the principles and administration of criminal law" would be introduced to correct "ethical and judgmental divergencies" occurring within the justice system.

"But meantime somebody, somewhere, had taken note of those four sex offenders' lenient sentences and had taken them to heart," Fortini said. "I made an exhaustive search of the papers and magazines of that period, and I found that any time there was an article or news story dealing with the alleged softening in the legal system, the same four cases got quoted. No one connected with the writing or publishing of the stories could have realised, of course, that they were fanning a flame that was going to flare into multiple slaughter."

So now the cases were firmly linked, and a straightforward hypothesis could be made concerning the motive—that is, the four sex offenders had, in the view of many people, been treated too leniently by the law, and someone had taken countermeasures.

"I spent a long weekend away at a hotel by Lake Como," Fortini said. "I took with me two bags packed with the personal effects the four murdered men had brought with them from prison. I spent three days going through the stuff."

Victim A, 45 years old, a bricklayer, had a paperback collection of western novels by Zane Grey. He also collected photographs of famous sportsmen. He had a two-volume journal of his day-to-day life in prison which was incredibly dull, recording the same morning-to-night time-table of events over and over, without any commentary to add colour or reveal anything about himself. His other property included a wristwatch engraved to him from his mother on his sixteenth birthday, and a framed photograph of his estranged wife.

"I opened the frame and looked behind the picture, which can be a revealing thing to do," Fortini said. "I found six obscene photographs of little girls."

Victim B, a street vendor who was 32 at the time of his death, had a collection of international postage stamps in one album and international banknotes in another. He had two pulp novels, both of them detective stories, a number of polished pebbles in a jar, and a dried frog to be worn as an amulet against illness.

The property of victim C was the bulkiest of the four. He had been a man of 60, a retired teacher, by all accounts fastidious in his manner and in his personal hygiene. His 300-page prison journal was written in a meticulous round hand, and on almost every page he took space to complain about the awfulness of the other men he was forced to live with. *They stink,* he wrote, *and they are just as foul and careless in their speech and in the way they behave towards each other. Little better than animals, and much less likeable.* His other belongings included a three-dimensional model of the Periodic Table, copies of *Galen's Anatomy*, Giuseppe di Lampedusa's novel *The Leopard*, and a Russian-language edition of Tolstoy's *Anna Karenina*; there were also four part-written manuscripts—one was a novel, one a treatise on female psychology (he hated women; he only attacked them, according to his journal, because they were "the necessary receptacles of man's carnal effluent"), the third was a travel book about southern Italy and Sicily, and the fourth was the first sixty stanzas of an epic poem with himself as the central heroic-tragic figure.

Victim D, by contrast, appeared to have been as basic as a man can be and still walk upright. He was a shop assistant, 29 when he died, who had kept a number of pocket-size pornographic magazines dismantled and concealed between the pages of a Bible; he also had a notebook filled with all-but illiterate pencilled details of rapes he would like to commit on famous women, with crude illustrations alongside, and a packet of twenty-six letters from a woman who signed herself *Anita*. His only other property was a cigarette lighter that doubled as an obscene novelty, and a 30-gram block of cannabis resin.

"From an investigative point of view," Fortini said, "the most interesting items were the twenty-six letters in the property of Victim D, whose name was Luigi. The dates suggested that the first letter was received a month after he was put in prison. All of the letters were written in green ink in a clear, confident hand; they were skilfully coy and suggested the author was rather more intelligent and guileful than she pretended to be. There were no envelopes with any of the letters, so we had no record of their source."

The first letter thanked Luigi for replying. Anita introduced herself as a 27-year-old blonde from Rimini, now living in northern Italy, where she worked as a hotel receptionist. She spent a paragraph explaining how she was drawn to the plight of men suffering imprisonment, and admitted there was something in the details of Luigi's case—and his photograph in the papers—that made her want to meet him when he got out. The letter continued for three pages in a part-coquettish, part candid vein, hinting at powerful sexual undertones in Anita's attraction to Luigi, and ended with a request that he reply as soon as he could, because she so looked forward to hearing from him. A postscript, heavily underlined, asked him to destroy the letter after he had read it, as she didn't want her

words, intended for him alone, to be seen by any other
man, in or out of that prison. The same plea appeared
at the end of the other twenty-five letters.

"I was intrigued," Fortini said. "The first letter in
the collection thanked Luigi for replying. But to what?
She had obviously made the first move. How?"

Prompted by Fortini, Detective Lattes made enquiries at the prison where Luigi served his sentence. He
was given permission to talk to prisoners who had
shared a cell with Luigi.

"The mystery of the penfriend's introduction was
soon cleared up," Lattes said, "or at least we had an
explanation. It didn't point us in any clear direction,
but it suggested a line of enquiry."

Two prisoners recalled that during a visiting session at the prison, Luigi was approached by a man
who introduced himself as a prison visitor, someone
who spent time with prisoners who otherwise would
have no one coming to see them.

"He sat with Luigi for ten minutes," the prisoner
said, "and just before he left he gave him a folded
slip of paper and told him if he wrote to that address
he would be sure of a warm response."

Luigi showed the paper to his cellmates, but he
wouldn't let any of them read it. He committed the
details to memory then destroyed the paper, so only
he would know the address.

Fortini said, "The question that confronted us now
was, did this correspondence have any significance?
Was it related in any way to the fact that Luigi wound
up in a gutter two days after being released from

prison, castrated, and with his knees shattered?"

Lattes felt it would be worthwhile following up the correspondence: "Being realistic, what else could we do? We had nothing else to go on."

Fortini felt that was a wise move, too. "In the meantime," he said, "I decided I would subject the letters to every kind of scientific scrutiny I could think of."

Lattes went back to the prison, and he took a police artist with him. Three inmates who remembered the prison visitor gave the artist their impressions of his build and facial features, and after three hours he had produced two detailed sketches that the prisoners agreed looked very much like the man. He was tall, thickset and balding, with a fringe of white hair and a thick white moustache. No one had ever seen him at the prison before, and he had not been seen there since.

"At this stage, as we were preparing copies of the drawings back at the station," Lattes said, "Dr. Fortini called me and suggested I go to the other three prisons, show the pictures around, and see if anybody remembered seeing the man."

The surprise upshot, Lattes said, was that the man had been seen at the other three prisons, and only once at each. He was remembered principally because of his distinctive bulk and the particularly rich white moustache. That worried Lattes, who began to suspect the moustache was a disguise, the kind designed to draw attention to itself and thereby diminish any clear recollection of the wearer's other distinguishing features—such as his voice.

"No one could recall hearing him speak, although three prisoners said they were at adjacent tables. They probably did hear his voice, but the dominant recollection was that damned moustache."

It was soon established that the mysterious visitor had given all four of the murder victims a slip of paper with the recommendation that they write to the address on it. Fortini wondered if the notably difficult victim C, the teacher, would have been tempted to write, given his aloofness from other people, and his well-documented dislike of women.

"But it occurred to me that the details of his curious psychology were a matter of public record," Fortini said. "The snobbishness, the misogyny, it had all been in the papers. The person known to us as Anita was clever enough, I guessed, to use her knowledge of victim C's personality to fashion a come-on that would be tailored to make him respond."

No one involved in the investigation doubted, now, that the letter-writer was the key to the killings. "But our certainty wasn't based on any great weight of evidence," Lattes said. "It was just getting obvious, that was all. As a suspected area of significance, it felt right."

Fortini, meanwhile, had a problem with the letters. While waiting for the results of various tests that he had set in motion, he read all twenty-six again, and concluded there was at least one missing.

"I was sure it had to be the last one. Unfortunately

the last two letters in our possession weren't dated, so we had no way of knowing how close to the time of Luigi's release they were sent. However, the series very neatly put on the pressure, building it month by month so that by the time the release date was in sight, a meeting between Anita and Luigi would be the inevitable next move. It would be the only thing he could think of.

"She told him how warm she got just thinking about him, and how the sight of his photograph was enough to make her tremble. She said she undressed in front of it every night before going to bed. Powerful stuff for a sex criminal who had been locked away for nearly two years. The question of a meeting was pointedly broached in letters 24, 25, and 26. It was definitely on the cards, yet a time and venue were never set. There *must* have been another letter."

Lattes agreed. He went back to the prison and asked to speak to Luigi's cellmates again. He spoke to them individually, explaining that he now knew part of the correspondence was missing. He told each in turn that he suspected one of the cellmates had stolen it.

"There was nothing brilliant in guessing that might be the answer," Lattes said. "In prison, one of the commonest felonies is the theft of one man's love letters by another. Especially if they're rich in sexual content. Dr. Fortini and I guessed that by the time Anita sent the last letter, she would have been pretty explicit in her predictions of how their first meeting would go."

To encourage the cellmates to violate one another's privacy, Lattes told each that there would be a little concession available to whoever turned up the missing correspondence.

"We don't know to this day which of them had the letter, but one of them handed it over less than twenty-four hours after I spoke to them. He got his concession—an extra ounce of tobacco a week for two months, courtesy of *Polizia Centrale* detectives' petty cash—and we got the missing link."

The final letter was certainly explicit, Fortini said. Not only sexually, but in the directions it gave Luigi. He was told where to go, what date, and at what time. Because it was not discreet just yet for anyone to be seen going to Anita's apartment, she explained, she would meet Luigi by the canal in the upper town at Bergamo.

"And that was where he died," Fortini said. "At that spot, on that date, at the appointed time."

Lattes now turned to Fortini for the next move. They had done all the divination and the *modus operandi* of a murderous scam had been immaculately deduced, but unfortunately it did not lead them to a suspect.

"That was when Dr. Fortini showed me that he had not been wasting his time," Lattes said. "He had already done pioneering work on a phenomenon he called fibre memory. It was developed much further in later years, but at that time, for all its crudity, it was revolutionary. I was so impressed I remember yelping with pleasure at the results."

What Fortini had done was to subject the top sheet of every letter to crosslight photography. This meant they were photographed with the light source—a harsh, focused projector beam—striking the surface of the paper almost at right angles.

"This threw up the texture of the paper and made it look like woolly blankets when the pictures were enlarged," Fortini said. "I had the top sheets photographed in each case because the pages were folded backwards from the front, which meant that the post office franking stamp, when it struck the envelope, would leave an impression on either the top or the lower half of the first page. The fibre of the letter would thereby retain a memory of the stamp, an indented duplicate of the postmark. It would be softer-edged than the mark on the envelope, of course, but my hope was that with appropriate treatment, we could make it legible."

Fortini recalled that a stage had been reached where he might have appeared to be showing off. "My mistake, if there was one," he said, "was to have set so much in motion without telling anyone in *Polizia Centrale*. It wasn't done by design, though. I was in the grip of my enthusiasm. Such a state kills my awareness of other things, other refinements of behaviour, other protocols. I might say it's the same condition of mind that helped destroy my marriage. What happened was, I saw a line of procedure stretching out in front of me, and I followed it without looking to left or right."

"I didn't think he was showing off," Lattes said. "I

was too grateful to think any such thing. He called in a photographic expert from Milan, which was a hell of an achievement in itself, and between them they got a photographic reproduction off three of those letters that confirmed the place of posting. It was Cremona, about 100 kilometres south of Bergamo. I was elated that Dr. Fortini had done this, but I found myself staring at him, silently asking him, what now?"

Fortini had an answer. It had been a question until twenty minutes before he showed Lattes the results of the postmark tests. Confirmation came directly from an official at the Criminal Identification Centre in Rome.

"The postmark on the letters," Fortini explained, "was obtained by enlarging the image of the faint imprint and making it as contrasty as possible in the printing process, so that shadows turned inky black and highlights came out snow white. That way we got the definition we needed to enable us to read the imprint. Well, I used the same technique to check the letters for fingerprints."

He had known it was another long shot, but he believed he had to try everything, since even if he identified the postmark, it would fall very short of identifying the murderer.

"Before I photographed the fingerprints—which were surprisingly clear under oblique light—I dusted them with a fine graphite powder."

The black graphite stuck to the latent traces of oil deposited by the fingers of those who had handled the letters. From the start, the police and Fortini had han-

dled the sheets with gloves. Fortini knew that nothing
in prison is guarded more closely than personal correspondence, so in his estimation, only two other
people were likely to have handled the letters without
gloves—the writer of the letters, and Luigi. Nevertheless, handling by other inmates was always a possibility; if it had happened, their prints would have to
be identified and eliminated.

"Luigi's prints were eliminated, and the experts in
Rome were able to determine that there was, indeed,
only one other set of prints on the letters. Fortunately,
too, the paper had been handled with some care, so
several very clear impressions had been left. The photographs, magnified 8 times, made the configuration
of the prints very clear. They were large male fingerprints."

Fortini hardly dared ask the next question: was
there a match for those fingerprints in the criminal
files?

"Yes, indeed, the official told me. My heart leapt.
I could scarcely believe it—the identity of the other
person who handled the letters, the person who *wrote*
them, was on record at the fingerprint centre. It was
a man called Alfonso Erba."

The record showed that Erba had been convicted
of serious assault on a convicted child molester seven
years previously. Fortini asked if a picture was on file.
Rome confirmed that they did have front and side
views of Alfonso Erba's face. Copies were put in the
mail that afternoon.

"And I thought Detective Lattes would start singing

when we opened the envelope next day. We took a cut-out white moustache, copied from one of the police artist's drawings of the prison visitor, and stuck it over the strong-featured, bald-headed image of Alfonso Erba. *Ecce!* It was our man, without a shadow of a doubt."

When Lattes travelled to Cremona later that day and went to the house of Alfonso Erba, he encountered no resistance to his questions. Erba simply shrugged and admitted that he wrote the letters—and yes, he killed the four men.

"He was incredibly self-possessed," said Lattes. "I don't think he was so paranoid as to see himself as an avenging angel, but he certainly believed he had done what needed to be done."

Erba told Detective Lattes that he knew the kind of weak men he was dealing with. He had been confident from the start that fervid appeals to their lack of character would work. He knew that even the pompous teacher, victim C, for all his protestations to nobility, was just another pervert.

"They had it coming," Erba told the detective. "I watched them die and I felt my niece's spirit liberated by their agony. I would do it again."

It transpired that the woman Luigi killed had been the niece of Alfonso Erba.

"For a long time he had suffered a righteous wrath at the lenient sentences handed out to sexual criminals," Lattes said. "When his niece died at the hands of a sexual deviate, his anger was compounded to the point where murder became an imperative."

Erba was charged, tried and given three life sentences. He died in prison ten years later, completely unrepentant.

In retrospect, Fortini finds the case satisfactory from the standpoint of deductive investigation, and for its scientific challenge at a time when electron microscopes and computers were tools that still lay in the future. He does admit, nevertheless, that the case hinged on various pieces of luck. Without the luckiest break of all, he would never have been able to get the investigation moving.

"It was just a good thing that Luigi didn't destroy the letters, as he was asked to. If he had done that, as the others obviously did, Alfonso Erba would probably have carried on luring sex criminals to their messy deaths until he got tired of it. Or until he got too old to hold a razor steady."

SIX

EGO TRIPPER

I used to argue that crime situations with high drama and solid plot occurred only in fiction," said Dr. Robert Trent, one-time forensic scientist with the Department of Forensic Examination of the New York Police Department. "I had no problem with that. It wasn't anything I resented, it was simply an observation. If people got diversion from murder stories where an intensely brilliant killer manages to wipe out half a community without leaving a clue, and only stops when a dazzlingly smart detective catches him, well OK. Those stories are attractive, they glamorise the felon to some extent and make a superman of the investigator. They create the unreal notion that serious crime can exist at a glitzy level, that there is such a thing as criminal chic."

Trent's first five years of professional experience had convinced him that crime, particularly murder, was essentially squalid.

"The unwashed smell of a day-old corpse summed it up for me. That was murder, that was the whole criminal arena, a stinky morass, populated by largely banal, uninteresting people with no subtlety and no mechanisms for picking up nuance in human affairs. I was aware there were occasional exceptions, but I was also aware the exceptions underscored the rule."

While Dr. Trent never did change his mind about the essential squalor and sleaziness of the average murder, he did become involved in a case that broadened his outlook at a single stroke.

"It had the stuff of pulp crime—weirdness, deep mystery, and a nice old-fashioned detective running the show. At the same time, the whole case was so unreal you could have made a musical out of it."

The dual murders of millionaire manufacturer Morton Conroy, 65, and his wife Valerie, 58, held the attention of press and public for a couple of days in October 1979. Conroy's face was known to most Americans—he appeared on billboards and in magazines all over the USA, advertising his popular range of home barbecue equipment. His wife was well known, too, from the regular television appeals she made as president of a foundation providing free medical care to the pets of the unemployed and people on low incomes.

The couple had been found dead, both shot through the heart, in the television room in their home at the

Hamptons, Long Island. Apart from the predictable stir created by the violent death of rich, socially prominent people, this case had several extra spins that guaranteed the full attention of the media.

"I was 30 years old at the time and probably still impressionable," Dr. Trent said, "although I thought of myself as cynical and quite immune to shock. The truth was, I didn't know until then what real shock was. The Conroy case was one of the most outstanding enquiries I ever got involved with, and it was one where I'm proud to say the forensic guys took hold of the reins and kept a grip on them till the investigation was complete."

The Conroys had died in a room without windows which was locked from the inside.

"Pure Agatha Christie," Trent said. "Except that when it's real, when you stand there, looking at the two bodies on the couch, hands folded in their laps, you realise you're at the centre of a profound mystery and there isn't the same quaint air of puzzle about it. We were dumbfounded. The detective running the case, Lieutenant Merrick, kept walking round the room, shrugging, then stopping in front of me and my colleagues and throwing us a questioning look. It was hard to know where to begin."

Merrick is now retired and intends to recount the story of the Conroy murders in a book he is writing about his career with the New York Police Department. Nevertheless he was not reticent about the case and was happy to pass on his recollections.

"The first thing I remember," he said, "was the

smell in that room. The door had been open maybe an hour by the time I got there. But the smell was still rich in the air, not powerful or overpowering or anything like that, but something distinctive, a part of the atmosphere. I found out later it was the smell of a scented Dutch cigar."

The smell was one of the minor mysteries surrounding the case. There were no cigars or cigar butts in the room where the couple died. It was known that Morton Conroy had never smoked, neither had his wife. They were not simply abstainers, they actively disliked tobacco and never allowed anyone to use it in their home.

"But that was nothing, compared to the other stuff that began turning up," Dr. Trent said. "I knew within minutes that this was going to be something spectacular, something on the symphonic scale of crime, the kind I hadn't believed existed. In parallel with the police, I began setting up my own investigation, running it alongside the routine duties I had to perform as a member of the forensic team."

Trent assembled the basic facts of the case from witness statements and from snippets of talk among the members of the police investigation team. The door to the room where the Conroys were found had been forced open by a police officer, after the maid called to him and his partner as they drove past in their squad car. The officers later reported that the maid, Harriet Mason, was nervous, and she appeared to be on the verge of tears. She explained that her employers had gone into the television room at approximately 11 o'clock the evening before.

"Mrs. Conroy told me I could go to bed," she said in her statement. "I tidied up in the kitchen and turned in at about 11:20. When I got up again at seven I prepared a light breakfast for them as I always do, then at 7.30 I pressed the bell-push in the kitchen that let them know their eggs, toast and coffee were waiting for them in the dining room. That was how they liked it, they would go in there and help themselves. I didn't usually see either of them until the afternoon, at the earliest. That suited me, they were both kind of snappish people until late afternoon, when they'd had a drink."

At 8:45 Harriet realised the Conroys still hadn't come down to breakfast. She panicked. Her first thought was that something had gone wrong with the bell-push in the kitchen. Although the Conroys habitually rose early, they relied on the maid to wake them. Harriet believed it was wholly likely that the bell hadn't worked and the couple had slept on.

"I'd no idea what to do for the best. They didn't like me coming to the bedroom door. Mrs. Conroy told me it made her feel invaded. I was always to use the internal telephone if I wanted her during the day or evening, or the bell to wake them. That was all. No visits in person. But when I tried the phone I got no answer. I could hear it ringing up there in the bedroom, and it would have wakened them because it was louder than the bell from the kitchen."

Harriet finally mustered the courage to go up and knock on the bedroom door. She knocked three times, rather hard the third time. When there was still no response she became seriously worried. She opened the door and looked in. There was no one in the room and the bed was still made up.

"I went downstairs, thinking how odd it was, them going out like that without waking me or letting me know in advance. Then I saw the television room door was shut. That wasn't normal. They always left it open because Mrs. Conroy complained the air in there got stale if it was left shut up overnight."

Harriet tried the door, found it locked, and at approximately the same time she heard the voice of a newscaster from inside the room. The television was still switched on.

"It dawned on me they could still be in there. I banged on the door but I got no reply. I went upstairs again and looked in the linen baskets in the bedroom. They hadn't undressed the night before, the baskets were empty. That was when I started to panic. I ran downstairs, banged on the TV room door again and still got nothing. I went to the hall, wondering if I should call the police, and then I looked out the window and saw the police car coming along the road."

An inspection of the door was made by Dr. Trent and a technician who specialised in the examination of lock mechanisms and safes. The brass key was still in the door lock, on the inside, where the maid said it always was. Trent removed it carefully and took several close-up photographs.

"I'd no idea what I was looking for," he said, "but there was this rule I had, and I stuck to it throughout my career; I even had it on a card pinned to the wall of my lab—*Look Under Every Stone*. If it was possible to do something with a piece of evidence, even if all I could think of was to take a picture of it, then I'd do that. The idea was literally to leave no stone unturned. Do everything, however fruitless or pointless the procedure might look."

The forensic team made a twofold sweep of the room, which meant they moved through it in two rows, one behind the other, lifting loose fibres from the carpets and furniture, dusting for prints, collecting any debris and bagging it.

"And in the meantime," Trent said, "the bodies were removed to the Medical Examiner's mortuary and autopsies were carried out. I went along and watched. I was glad I did. Ten minutes into the autopsy on Morton Conroy, the pathologist looked up at his partner and said, 'This is fucking crazy.'

"I moved nearer the table and the pathologist looked at me. 'Crazy,' he said again. I asked him what was up. He pointed into the open abdomen in front of him. 'A direct bullet wound to the heart. Powder burns and muzzle bruising on the site of entrance. The heart is torn open at the left ventricle. That adds up to an efficient piece of homicide with a firearm, as such things go. Only there's no bullet.' "

The pathologist's assistant had a look, but he couldn't find a bullet either. They abandoned Morton Conroy's body and together they opened the body of his wife Valerie, which lay on the adjacent table.

"They dug into her very carefully for a couple of

minutes," Trent said, "following the track of the bullet down to the heart. Then the pathologist looked over at me again; 'Ditto,' he said. There was no sign of a bullet."

Young Dr. Trent was intrigued with this development. He went back to his own laboratory and sat gazing down the eyepiece of a microscope. There was nothing under the microscope; this was one of the ways he could concentrate on a problem without being interrupted.

"I decided to stick with my dictum and do all the testing possible to everything I could get my hands on. There had to be answers in this case, even if someone seemed intent on making it hard for us to find them. I called the pathology lab and asked if I could collect tissue samples from the bodies of the Conroys. They said sure. So I went to the morgue and excised what I needed from the bodies. I took several of the portions of tissue to the metallurgy lab and filled out a request. At the histology lab I handed over the remaining tissue and filled out another request. Then I went back to the Conroys' house to see how things were going with the police investigation.

"I spoke to Lieutenant Merrick, who confessed he was moving forward with the sense of getting further and further into the dark. Nothing he had discovered, so far, had told him any more about the case, and he didn't believe he had any views or theories that would stand up to scrutiny. When I told him there were no bullets in the Conroys' bodies, he nodded, as though

I had confirmed at least one point on which he had an opinion."

Lieutenant Merrick recalled that moment. "I said to Dr. Trent, 'This is all a game some bastard is playing.' I was at least sure of that. The locked door, the cigar smoke, no bullets in the bodies—it wasn't anything like a real murder case. It was a travesty, a stage play, and I felt it had all been engineered to annoy the hell out of the police. We were busy people, *stressed* people. We had better things to do than hang around trying to solve puzzles."

Trent remembered thinking that the travesty, as Merrick called it, was more like someone trying to prove how clever he was. "I could understand an overworked police officer, under pressure to get results, getting mad at the apparent mockery of the details in the case, but to me it was a challenge. I told myself I was going to get to the bottom of this thing and crack it."

Trent turned his attention to the maid, Harriet. While she was down at the station answering routine police questions, he went back to the house, went straight to Harriet's room, and began a methodical search. He did not suspect her of anything at that point, but she was the only person left alive at the Conroy household, so in his estimation it made sense to know all he could about her.

"My approach was described as amoral by one of my superiors at the time," Trent said. "He was probably right, but it's an amoral world and I *was* investigating a double murder, so what the hell? If I didn't find something significant, something incriminating or at least suspicious, no one besides myself would know I'd violated Harriet's privacy. In a perfectly real sense, no harm would be done."

But he did find something. At a superficial level of search Harriet's room and her belongings presented a model of chaste tidiness or, as he called it, "demure order." The second level of search, which involved looking in places where people would not usually keep or conceal things, presented a very different picture.

"She had three small suitcases," Trent said, "all with false bottoms, and all packed with hundred-dollar bills, more than a thousand of them. There was also a box in one of the false cavities; inside it was a pair of forceps with the gripper jaws on the ends turned over at right angles, a blue canister with some kind of liquid inside, and a partly burned cigar.

"Two pairs of shoes had heels that swivelled aside to reveal cavities, and inside the cavities there were necklaces, a couple of really delicate wrist watches and three diamond rings. Even her coin purse had a false pocket, and in there I found three photographs: one showed Harriet and a young man, dressed identically in cowboy suits and holding revolvers in the air; the second was a shot of the same young man in a wheelchair, and the third showed Harriet sitting by a hospital bed in which the young man was propped up, looking desperately ill. I photographed everything I had found so far, put it all back, and completed my search in the bathroom adjoining Harriet's bedroom.

In the space behind the washbasin I found a Smith and Wesson revolver, wrapped in plastic."

Trent tried to call Lieutenant Merrick, but he was in court on a separate matter and couldn't be reached. A call to Merrick's superior, Captain Howson, produced such a hostile reaction that Trent decided against telling the man anything. Instead, he went back to the Department of Forensic Investigation and checked the results of the tissue tests performed by the metallurgy and histology laboratories.

"I believed that I now had most of the picture," Trent said. "I took a taxi out to the court building where Merrick was detained and I managed to locate one of his team, Sergeant Lomax. I told him he should keep an eye on Harriet, I believed she had reason to skip. I told him I also had reason to believe before she skipped, she would brazen her way through the whole investigation, then vanish without a spot of suspicion attaching to her. But why take the risk?

"Well, to put it in an understated way, Sergeant Lomax thought I was hallucinating. His attitude, I may say, was symptomatic of a problem I had at the time but which disappeared a few years later—I looked like a juvenile, a witless juvenile at that, and people found it hard to believe I could locate my own ass with a torch and a map. The idea of me solving a crime was not one that many people could support."

Lomax told Trent that the maid had been cleared of suspicion at a very early stage. Her answers to questions all checked out, and her background details were confirmed on a telex received from the police in her home town in Maine. Her room had been carefully searched by detectives and found to be above suspicion. All in all Harriet was probably the cleanest, most law-abiding citizen Sergeant Lomax had met in a month.

"In addition to Lomax's distrust of my callow looks and manner," Trent said, "I detected a trace of Captain Howson's dislike of scientists. Policemen in America, it has to be said, do not often think forensic workers are anything better than bumbling auxiliaries, hamstrung with too many theories and starved of common sense. I looked at Lomax's condescending, pitying sneer, and suddenly I felt too disheartened to try any more. I decided to forget the warnings. If Harriet skipped, she skipped. I would wait until the sensible and intelligent Lieutenant Merrick was available, then I would tell him what I knew."

It was a further ten hours before Merrick showed up at Trent's office. He was tired, unshaven and short-tempered. He told Trent that he had to agree with his sergeant—the maid was not even a candidate for suspicion, and he would take some convincing to believe she was.

"I truly felt that Dr. Trent had gone way over the edge on this one," Merrick recalled. "But he was patient, he got me a beer, sat me down by his desk and pulled this folder full of papers over in front of him. He gave it to me nice and slowly. First he told me about the search he had done in Harriet's room, and he showed me the pictures he took. Right there, all the wind went out of my sails. I mean my men had checked that room. They had performed a thorough professional search. I felt like going out, finding them, and shooting them."

"I could see he was embarrassed," Trent said. "But I wasn't doing this to embarrass him. I had all the material he needed to build a case. I was about to hit him with the real stuff, the heavy scientific artillery, but he stopped me. He had to go, he said. He had to arrest that little lady right away."

Merrick took Harriet Mason into custody and impounded the evidence Trent had found. He filled out an arrest report, drank three cups of coffee one after the other, then called Trent and asked him if he would mind coming over to the police station.

"I was expecting some feedback from my boss," Merrick said, "as soon as they could rouse him from whatever bed he was in that night. He would be mad and sceptical and all kinds of other things, and I wanted to savour all that while it was fresh. You will gather, I did not like my boss. He was a shit, God rest his soul."

Trent arrived at the station house at four in the morning. In an interview room he sat opposite Merrick and put the scientific evidence to him.

"He hadn't been expecting anything half as good, half as powerful," Trent said. "First, I told him about the locked door to the Conroys' television room. I had studied the key, so had my colleague who specialised in locks and keys, and we had both noticed that on the end of the brass shaft, there were small, fresh abrasion marks. Later, when I found the forceps with the right-angled jaws, I could see flecks of brass glinting in the perforations at the tips. My associate told me it was an old device, used at one time by burglars. When a room was locked from the inside, the forceps were pushed through the keyhole from the outside of the door; they gripped the end of the key, which could then be turned by applying simple leverage to the handles of the forceps.

"But instead of using the forceps to open the door, Harriet had used them to lock it from outside, thus making it look as if it had been locked on the inside."

Merrick said he had trouble containing himself. He couldn't wait to start questioning Harriet, but he would wait all the same. "I was enthralled," he said. "Dr. Trent's enthusiasm, which was quite boyish in those days, conveyed everything graphically—I could see the bitch on her knees, turning those forceps in the lock.

"But that was only a tiny revelation in a whole damn sea of mysteries. I tried not to interrupt Dr. Trent, but I had to, I couldn't help myself. What was she doing it for, I asked him, and what about the murders, and the fact there were no bullets in the bodies? I suddenly needed to know everything at once."

Trent first explained that Harriet, for reasons yet to be discovered, had decided to kill the Conroys. She had two lines of attack, and she had probably preferred the less violent one over the other, although she couldn't be too sure it would work. First, she had opened the humidifier into the television room and filled it with the substance from the blue canister; the substance was trichlorethylene, an industrial solvent which is also a powerful anaesthetic.

"It probably knocked them out quite fast," Trent said, "but the chances of it killing them, even in an unventilated room, were slight. She would have needed a much bigger vaporiser. Samples of brain tissues showed a slight concentration of the chemical, but not enough to kill an adult.

"So after a while, when Harriet checked on the Conroys to see if they had died, she would have realised they were simply asleep, and were likely to wake up in a worse mood than usual, unless she did something else. So Plan B was put in operation. Vanishing bullets."

Merrick said he had heard of ice being used as bullets, which melted and left no trace, but he had been told by many experts that such devices would only work in one or two cases out of ten. "When he said vanishing bullets, I had no idea what he meant. But then he showed me. He had made one. It was the usual shell case with the powder charge inside, packed on top of the detonator, but instead of a lead bullet, there was a small chunk of pork spare rib. So help me. He had cut it to shape and it was really compact and hard."

Trent explained that the meat bullet, with its bony component, would easily penetrate a human chest if it was fired at close quarters, and it would do much the same internal damage as a dumdum bullet. By the time it had ploughed through the heart, it would be fragmented and indistinguishable from the fat, rib, muscle and connective tissue it had torn apart.

"Tissue samples checked in the histology lab confirmed it," Trent said. "There was pork and pork-rib tissue present in the chest wounds in both victims."

Merrick admitted that for a while he was simply speechless. So much information flooding in on him, after the case had promised to yield so little, was a shock to the system. He sat staring at his clasped hands on the table, then after a while he looked up. "What was the cigar smoke all about?" he asked Trent.

"To cover the smell of the trichlorethylene, I think," Trent said.

"But why, for Christ's sake, did she go to all that elaborate trouble?"

Trent remembered that, at that point, he tried not to sound too smug. "That's the little bit *you* have to find out," he said.

Merrick interviewed Harriet the following morning. When she was confronted with the weight of evidence she put up no resistance.

"I always said I'd admit everything, if I had to," she told Merrick. "I didn't think I'd have to, though. You have to agree that was pretty clever stuff I did."

"Not clever enough," Merrick said, "and far too elaborate."

Harriet nodded. "It wasn't meant to go the way it did. What I had there were a few alternatives, and I just ended up using more of them than I should."

Merrick asked her why she killed her employers.

"Because they killed my brother."

"Is he the young man in the photographs?"

"Harvey Mason, 23 years old. A real nice fella in lots of ways, a fine mechanic, too, a champion shot, amateur escapologist . . ." Harriet sighed. "A barbecue gas tank blew up in his face. A *Conroy* barbecue tank. It didn't kill him straight away. He looked set to recover, but there was nerve damage. He got some kind of galloping sclerosis of the spine and brain stem. Died a miserable death."

Merrick asked if Harriet or her family had sued the Conroy organisation.

"Oh sure. They spent more on lawyers than it would have cost to compensate three Harveys for the harm done, and for their money they got a not-guilty verdict."

"So you decided to get even."

"I decided to do a lot of things Harvey and me talked about when we were these wild inventive teen-agers. Harvey was a fan of Houdini. I mean a real fan. It was nearly an obsession with him. He learned all the stunts. Could get out of a straitjacket in two minutes, out of a milk churn full of water in three. He invented things. He invented the beef bullets— that's what they were at the start, bits of beef with shards of bone mixed in."

Merrick wasn't going to argue with someone making a full confession, but he knew that the meat bullet idea was devised by a Mafia Consigliere in Salerno in the 1950s. He knew it because Dr. Trent had told him.

"Why did you do all that stuff, really?" Merrick

asked. "Was it an ego trip? Were you demonstrating all the clever shit you could do?"

"That was part of it," Harriet said, "but the whole thing about it was, I got confused. I was set on killing those two but I hadn't worked out a straight-line plan. I was kind of banking on the chemical working, but at the same time I didn't trust it, you know?"

"Tell me about that."

"Well, the chemical poison I knew about from my uncle, who worked in a degreasing plant. He called the stuff trilene. He had seen a man keel over and die when he inhaled the vapour from the hot vats. My uncle used it to gas an old dog, too. That was 1953, or 1954. He'd kept a whole box of the canisters when he was kicked out of the job—it was great stuff for cleaning grease out of clothes, but I wasn't sure if it would still work as a poison after all that time. So I brought along one of Harvey's guns just in case. And I brought what he called his master cover device, the little scissors things that lock a door from the outside while the key's on the inside. That was another Houdini idea."

"Do you think," Merrick said, "that maybe you were trying to honour your brother by doing all this stuff—the door locking, the meat bullets . . ."

"Definitely. I had the half notion I was using his talents to get him his revenge."

"How did you get yourself into the Conroy household the way you did?"

"What I planned in the first place was to get a job in one of the factories here in New York, then I'd get close to the Conroys, one way or another, and I'd kill them. I mean there's no argument about it, they deserved to die. They were rotten people. Then when I was at their factory office there, ready to apply for a job in an assembly plant, I saw a job advertised for a maid. I asked the guy on the desk and he told me it was for the Conroys' own household; they wanted somebody to replace the old lady that had died a month before, and had been with the family forever. So I got some fake ID references put together, I applied for the job, and six weeks ago I got it."

Merrick asked her where she got the money that was hidden in her bags.

"The bags are great, aren't they?" she said. "Harvey made them."

"The money," Merrick pressed her. "Tell me about that."

"It came from the safe in the study," she said. "It was a pushover. It's English, pretty old, a John Tann four-corner bent-banded, with a German Hirschfeld combination lock. Harvey showed me how to open one of those when I was 16. And you know what? Old man Conroy had so much tucked away in there, he never even missed the fortune I took off him. Every week for five weeks I helped myself to just plenty. He didn't notice a thing, just kept sticking more in there. I took a lot of jewellery and stuff, too."

Merrick said he knew about that. "The business with the cigar," he said. "Was that to cover the smell of the chemical?"

"No, not really," Harriet said, "although I guess

that's the job it did. It was really to incriminate Howard Leavis."

"Who's Howard Leavis?"

"The asshole I talked to at the recruitment office, who treated me like something stuck on the heel of his shoe." Harriet shrugged. "It was kind of an afterthought. I stole one of his cigars to spite him, but later I thought there was a chance I could maybe, you know, get him in trouble up to his bumpers."

"But we didn't catch on to that clue. Tell me, Harriet, was all that stuff really a panic attack, some kind of jumbled response to the situation you were in?"

"You could say so. I'll tell you this, when you think you've got a solid plan lined up, a plan that can't possibly fail, that's the time to kick yourself and work out the alternatives, because chances are, it'll go belly up. To be honest, I didn't know what I was doing at the finish, I just tried everything, even the silly locked door thing, out of respect to Harvey—and hoped I'd get away with what I'd done."

"So," Merrick said, "the summing up is, you shot the Conroys in cold blood, while they were unconscious on their couch."

"No, it wasn't like that."

"Pardon me?"

"They kicked up all kinds of shit about the smell two minutes after I started the humidifier with the chemical in it. So they had breathed some, but they were *really* conscious when I walked in there and shot them. It wasn't horrible. They just dropped their heads and died, a lot more peacefully than poor Harvey."

The case against Harriet Mason did not endure as far as a trial. Because of a technical inaccuracy in the presentation of the prosecution case—four dates were misaligned, so they were wrongly applied to separate incidents cited in the indictment—the judge declared the case invalid. Harriet Mason went free.

Outside the court she told Lieutenant Merrick that she was happy with the way things had turned out. "It could have gone differently," she told him, "I could have had the money and the jewels, but the way it stands, I'm sure Harvey feels better now."

"And that's all that matters?" Merrick said.

"Absolutely, Lieutenant. He sees us both, and he's smiling."

SEVEN

RETRIBUTION

Crimes committed by psychotics are usually difficult to solve. A psychotic killer is likely to murder on impulse, and his victim is often a complete stranger; establishing a motive under those circumstances can be impossible. A psychotic criminal is also likely to be a superlative schemer who will spend considerable time on planning a crime and its concealment.

"Give me an ordinary villain any day of the week," said Inspector Antonio Moreno of the *Comisaria de Policia* at Zaragoza, in North Eastern Spain. "After I've been dealing with a psychotic or two, I always feel some affection for ordinary criminals. The difference between straightforward villains and psychot-

ics is, to me, like the difference between furry animals
and insects."

In the summer of 1992, in the town of Sariñena,
60 kilometres north-east of Zaragoza, the details of a
savage attack on a woman compelled Inspector Moreno to conclude that, once again, he would be chasing a psychotic. Shortly afterwards another woman
was attacked at a place close to Zaragoza. The features of the second attack made it clear the same man
had committed both crimes.

"The particular mental deformity this time around,"
Moreno said, "was sadism. I was chasing a sadist,
God help me. It was my first one ever, although by
that time I had gone after practically every other kind
of emotional freak. Until then, I don't think I had
quite understood the meaning of the term sadism, and
I certainly didn't know the terrible things a sadist will
do."

True full-blown sadism is a psychosexual disorder
where a person's sexual urges are satisfied by inflict-
ing pain on another person. The term Sadism was
introduced by a nineteenth-century German psychologist, Richard von Krafft-Ebing, and the name referred directly to the Marquis de Sade, a French
nobleman who wrote lengthy accounts of his own in-
dulgence in cruelty for sexual gratification. Sadism is
often linked to masochism, where sexual excitement
results from receiving pain. Some people, sadomaso-
chists, can respond in either role. The sadist, though,
will go for a victim who is not a masochist, because

a great deal of his sexual zest is derived from the victim's unwillingness.

The extent of sadistic violence varies, from the administration of mild pain to extreme cruelty, sometimes causing serious injury or death. The sadist's satisfaction may result from mental rather than physical pain in his victim. Sexual urges can diminish the level of violence in some sadists, but usually the aggressive impulse predominates and the sadist gives in to more and more extreme manifestations of his perverse tendencies. Sadism is a factor in many cases of rape and murder.

"I, for one, have always had difficulty believing in the sadistic personality as a disorder," said Dr. Ramon Aub, a consultant psychiatrist from Barcelona. "I can see that childhood influences may distort the development of the personality, and I do believe that certain types of disorder—I take the word disorder to mean a derangement or abnormality of function—can be brought about by outside pressures and events. But the notion that cruelty can be *implanted* in a person in these ways, the notion that it is some kind of illness, however caused, is a proposition I have battled in the past to understand, and nowadays I battle to denounce."

Dr. Aub, who was brought in as an expert adviser on the case described here, explained that among psychiatrists and others closely concerned with mental disturbance, there have always been two points of view about sadism. He quotes a celebrated trial of a

sadist in Germany, in 1979, which produced powerfully opposing opinions in the experts.

"The sadist in question was called Dieter Frink,"
Dr. Aub said. "At the time of his arrest he was described in the tabloid press as looking coarse and de-
generate, and having seen photographs of the man I
would say that was an accurate description. He was
charged at a court in München with the homicides of
ten women over an eight-week period. The murders
were the culmination of a grotesque criminal career
rooted in Frink's childhood in a poor southern suburb
of Berlin.

"At the trial, a criminologist put emphasis on the
fact that the prisoner had been brutally treated as a
child, and suggested he might not have led such a
downgrade adult life if his childhood had been even
slightly touched by the accepted standards of protec-
tion and care. A forensic psychiatrist and a clinical
psychologist went further: they put forward the view
that Frink would have grown into an ordinary con-
forming adult, with no special abnormalities in his
behaviour, had it not been for his bizarre upbringing.

"The psychiatrist said that beneath the grossness
and depravity infesting every level of the defendant's
view of life, there were lingering traces of normal
human impulses—decent human values, which had
been crippled and repressed by the hideous circumstances of his treatment as a child.

"Now it so happened that Hans Kuchelmann, a specialist in criminal psychology, read a newspaper report of the trial and wrote to a learned journal to

complain that the court was being misled by senti-
mental, wrong-headed assessments of a man who was
clearly bad and would never have been any better,
whatever the circumstances of his childhood."

Dr. Aub kept a copy of the letter Kuchelmann
wrote, and it is reproduced here:

Sirs: It is perfectly clear to anyone in day-to-day
contact with criminals that certain individuals
are structured to work against the prevailing mo-
rality. They are equipped with contrary instincts,
and so deviation and subversion are the characteristics of such persons, just as kindness and
good humour may be outstanding characteristics
of others. In-built features of a person's character should never be mistaken for distortions
brought about by environment or upbringing.
Such distortions exist, of course, but they are
never so prominent or extreme as the vicious
impulses and repugnant psychosexual traits exhibited by the defendant in this case. Dieter
Frink is not a sick man, he is a bad man. There
is no cure for his behaviour because it is not a
sickness, and he should not be represented to the
jury as a victim, when in fact he is decidedly a
cold-blooded victimiser on whom sympathy and
compassion would be wasted.

Professor Kuchelmann's views were never presented
to the court and were not published until after Frink's
trial, but a police witness called by the prosecution

did put forward a similar view in open court. When he was asked if he had ever come across anyone like Dieter Frink before, the officer said he never had.

"I have met men who have murdered children, and men who killed other people for money, but none of them were as cold as Frink. He gives the feeling that he's completely heartless, in fact not quite human."

The officer was asked whether, in his experience of dealing with people, he could identify Frink as being a man in need of any kind of help.

"He's not sick, if that's what you're asking," the officer said. "The sickness is in anybody who would believe that kind of garbage."

Dr. Aub felt he had to side with the views of Professor Kuchelmann and the police officer. "When I was called by Inspector Moreno and asked to give an evaluation of the person who had committed two very nasty crimes, I suppose I must have sounded rather strident and vindictive. I told him he was looking for an inverted freak who did not deserve an ounce of human sympathy. I told him many other things, all in the same vein. Later, over a drink, I explained to the good Inspector that sadists always have that effect on me. They are not sick, I told him, they are wicked."

Both crimes were unusually savage. In the first, a young schoolteacher on a sabbatical from Madrid was abducted in Sariñena in broad daylight. She was dragged backwards into the back of a van and blindfolded so she couldn't see her attacker. She was taken to a deserted farm cottage on the northern outskirts of the town. Once inside, she was stripped naked and

attacked with a sharp instrument, probably a razor.
Her lower abdomen and thighs were slashed numerous times. While she bled and cried with fright and
pain, her attacker raped her, then drove off and left
her in the cottage.

The victim's life was saved by a helicopter pilot.
He was flying low over the region when he saw her
clambering over the rocks, naked and bleeding from
her wounds. He landed the helicopter and ran to her.
She became hysterical, thinking her attacker had come
back. The pilot calmed her, wrapped her in a blanket
and flew her to hospital in Zaragoza.

"The second attack was even messier," Inspector
Moreno said. "A young mother, feeding chickens in
the yard behind her house, was grabbed from behind,
punched unconscious and blindfolded. She was bundled into the hen-house, tied to the spars with lengths
of wire, then had all her clothes torn off. She regained
consciousness as she was being raped. She began
screaming, but there was a sudden, terrible pain and
she couldn't make a sound any more, the pain was so
terrible, she said, that it constricted her throat. When
she thought she couldn't take the pain any more it
suddenly got worse and she passed out.

"She was found approximately an hour later by her
husband. A few minutes more and she might have
died. She had been cut in the same way as the schoolteacher, on the thighs and belly. A broom handle had
been pushed into her anus and the entire length of a
wooden trowel-handle had been forced into her vagina. Blood transfusions saved her life. In the weeks

following the attack she needed four operations to correct the internal damage to her lower body."

There were no suspects. The police made thorough searches at and around the scenes of both attacks, but they found no incriminating evidence.

"It was my view," said Dr. Aub, "that the sadist would attack again. It's in their nature. Some of them will wait a lifetime to commit that first act, and they may even die without ever plucking up the courage, but once they've begun, they will never stop unless they are compelled. And the crimes always get worse, the wickedness is always explored in broader and broader strokes.

"I recommended a forensic scientist to Inspector Moreno. He was José Pinillos, who for many years had made a speciality of hair and fibre analysis. If Moreno could persuade Pinillos to come in on the investigation, there was a chance it might develop in a positive direction."

José Pinillos was by that time retired, but when Moreno contacted him and gave him the details of the case, he said he would be happy to help in exchange for his expenses and the occasional bottle of wine.

"The occasional bottle meant at least two a day," said Inspector Moreno, "but he was worth it."

Pinillos was a faintly comic figure. He was very tall, gaunt featured and incredibly thin—so thin, in fact, that local people soon generated a rumour about him suffering from a terminal illness. He wore plaid shirts, faded jeans, sandals and a wide-brimmed straw hat, and looked more like an itinerant farm labourer than a forensic scientist.

"Within two days he had begun to collect evidence," Inspector Moreno said. "At the cottage where the teacher was attacked he found grey-green wool fibres on the floor and on the window ledge. They didn't tally with anything the teacher had worn that day, so there was a chance they had come from her attacker. Next morning, after crawling around for nearly two hours in the hen-house where the second victim was attacked, he came up with more fibres. They were very fine, but under his microscope he could see they were the same as the fibres he had found at the cottage."

Pinillos also began a painstaking search for fingerprints. He used a variety of techniques—low-tack adhesive tape for lifting prints, various coloured powders for detecting prints on different surfaces, plus a set of lamps with coloured filters, for examining rough or discoloured surfaces for the presence of prints.

"He was too calm and thorough to be called fanatical in his approach," Inspector Moreno said, "but there was something obsessive in the way he would not leave any possibility unexplored. On his fourth day with us, a messenger from Barcelona brought Pinillos a lifting kit, and he set to work at the cottage and the hen-house all over again."

The lifting kit is based around a machine which electrostatically charges a sheet of plastic, which can then lift indistinct footprints clean off a floor or any other surface. The image can then be isolated and photographed under whichever type of light throws up the most detail.

"He got three complete footprints—all from a right shoe. Two from the cottage, one from the hen-house. They were identical, and the shoe was a man's."

After making absolutely sure that the second victim's husband did not have shoes with a sole pattern the same as that on the prints, Pinillos had the prints made into photographs and blown up to triple size. He hung them in his centre of operations, a tiny office at the back of the *Comisaria de Policia* in Zaragoza.

"Pinillos was not an unfriendly man," Moreno said, "but he had a habit of lapsing into deep silences that lasted for hours. Another thing was he would make unexplained visits to the hospital, and appear with new specimens from the crime scenes without saying what they were. I had been told it was best to let him work to his own eccentric pattern, and I did that, though it was hard to keep my nose out of his business. As time passed I could tell he was concentrating, all the time concentrating, perhaps working to establish a procedural pointer that would dictate his next move."

Halfway through Pinillos's tenth day on the case, a report of another attack reached the station at Zaragoza. Inspector Moreno, José Pinillos and two junior detectives drove out to the crime scene, an abandoned wayside tool store.

"It was just a big concrete box," Moreno said, "with a small square door in the front, barely large enough to let a corpulent policeman like me slip inside. The interior was musty and completely dark. The victim had been found inside by an old man walking past—he heard her crying. He called an ambulance and then the police. By the time we got there she had been removed, of course, but the ambulance personnel had been careful to leave the scene undisturbed. Pinillos insisted that he be allowed to go in first, with his equipment.

"So he went in and we waited, and we could see his lights roaming the concrete walls from time to time, and we heard his camera clicking away, and there was the hum of the lifting kit and the clink and clatter of other instruments. Busy, busy, busy—which is gratifying when you are involved, when you're getting into the rhythm of a fast-forward investigation, but the three of us standing outside, waiting, felt like we were being excluded from the case. We remained patient, and after nearly an hour Pinillos emerged, wearing an uncharacteristic grin."

Pinillos had collected fibres, fingerprints, footprints and a semen sample. He put everything carefully into the back of the car, then said he would like to see the victim. The junior detectives sealed off the crime scene and they all drove out to the hospital.

"She was a terrible sight," Inspector Moreno said. "Only 16, a slender little thing, abducted on the way home from her second day in her very first job. She had been blindfolded so tightly there was a bruise running all the way across her eyes and round the sides of her face. Her attacker had punched her abdomen so hard that her liver was ruptured. She had been slashed at the thighs and belly, one of her nipples was sliced off, and after raping her he had shoved stones and earth into her vagina and anus."

While the victim was being prepared for surgery, José Pinillos examined her face for a few minutes, then gently took swabs from her cheeks and neck.

"The surgeon said there was time to take more specimens if he wanted to," Inspector Moreno said, "but Pinillos said no, he had enough."

The following day nobody saw much of Pinillos. He shut himself away in his little office with two bottles of wine, all his notes and his collection of specimens. Finally, that evening, he approached Inspector Moreno.

There had been a great deal for him to collate and tabulate, he explained, and much of it would only be of use for corroboration of police findings at a later time, but for the moment, he could offer Inspector Moreno an interim report.

The man they were looking for, he said, habitually wore the same grey-green wool trousers, and took a size ten in *Sandor* brand shoes, in the style called *Bronco*. He was approximately six feet tall, grey-haired, and used a cologne called *Orilla de Mar*. He was also asthmatic.

"I couldn't help smiling," Moreno said. "He sounded like Sherlock Holmes. I told him I didn't doubt for one moment that what he said was correct, but please, he had to tell me how he knew all that."

Pinillos explained. The grey-green fibres were from a batch of Indonesian-made trousers sold by three local branches of a chain store: 34 pairs had been sold within a 100-kilometre radius in the past six months, and the trousers were sold nowhere else in Spain.

The shoe size had been obtained from the footprints, the make and style were discovered by taking pictures of the sole around the shoe shops until a match was found.

"The estimation of height was cunning," Inspector Moreno said. "It seems that in cases of abduction and molestation, sometimes the woman's forehead will suffer a mild abrasion—this is caused by stubble on her attacker's chin. It had been established that an average-size woman, being manhandled by a man in the region of six feet tall, will have fine abrasions or reddening of the delicate skin of her forehead at, or near, the hairline. The estimation is confirmed by an equation involving the position of finger-grip marks on the arms, and bruising on the victim's legs from the attacker's knees.

"As for the hair colour, that was straightforward observation. It was noted from identical hair specimens found at all three crime scenes."

The cologne was identified from swabs taken from the faces of all three victims. "Pinillos detected the odour in the cottage, first of all," Moreno said, "and that alerted him to the possibility that a cologne was involved."

Pinillos sent the swabs to Madrid for ultra-sensitive chromatography testing—the process breaks down a substance into its components. The results showed it was a solution consisting of alcohol and 6 per cent perfume. The scent was derived from a mixture of citrus oils—lemon and orange—plus lavender and neroli. The analysis was checked against known formulae, and up came the match, a cologne called *Orilla de Mar*.

Inspector Moreno said that Pinillos had carried out an analysis on hair deposits from the victims' heads by soaking samples of hair in distilled water, then analysing the traces in the water. "Again, he got the same positive result from all three women. There was a chemical present, salbutamol sulphate, which is used in asthma inhalers. The attacker had breathed the stuff over the women's hair. Apparently this wasn't an unlikely discovery. Pinillos explained that rapists and other aggressive types who happen to be on respiratory medication often have to take a shot prior to making their move on a victim. They're so worked up that an asthma attack can be on the cards if they don't take steps to prevent it."

Moreno distributed the description of the attacker to outlying police stations. Pinillos, meantime, went around the pharmacies in the region.

"I saw no harm in letting him do that," Moreno said. "He was the one running the investigation, anyway. I could see he was enjoying himself, so I left him to get on with it."

On the second day of visiting pharmacies, Pinillos struck lucky at a small privately owned business in Zaragoza. A man answering the general description of the attacker regularly brought in a prescription for an asthma inhaler. The last time had been two weeks before, the pharmacist said, so the man was due back again soon.

"It was the kind of arrest a couple of boy scouts could have made," Moreno said. "For four days we sat in a car across the square from the pharmacy—me, two younger detectives and Pinillos. At about noon on the fifth day the man showed up. It was uncanny, he looked just the way Pinillos had described him. He was tall, grey, intense looking. I waited until he was inside the pharmacy, then I sent my boys in to pick him up. He came out with them without offering any resistance."

The suspect was Manuel Benavente, a cattle-feed distributor who lived alone on a farm two kilometres east of Zaragoza. At first he denied everything, but when Pinillos was allowed to present him with all the evidence he had collected, he stopped denying and demanded to speak to a lawyer instead. He had no legal representative of his own, so Moreno promptly appointed a local lawyer to defend him.

"Benavente was really shocked at the stuff Pinillos had on him," Moreno said. "Saliva samples, fingerprints, a DNA breakdown from the semen, skin scrapings from under the victims' nails, the wool fibres, the hair, the cologne, the asthma drug. In the end, Pinillos made it look as though Benavente had left every scrap of information about himself at the crime scene—everything but his name."

Pinillos even made a small joke on that point. He told Benavente he'd got his name from the women's hair.

Approximately six hours after his arrest, Manuel Benavente was formally charged with rape and serious assault on all three women. That evening, three hours after he had been locked up in a cell at the Zaragoza *Comisaria de Policia*, the lawyer came to see him, was shown into the cell and the door was locked behind him.

"The officer on duty had only got halfway back to the desk when he heard one of the men scream," Moreno said. "He ran back, opened the cell door, and saw the lawyer standing over the prisoner, who was writhing on the floor. His hands were clutching at his neck and blood was leaking between his fingers. His throat had been cut, ear to ear."

The lawyer turned calmly and handed the razor to the police officer. He stood by as while a doctor was called and remained impassive when he arrived. The doctor knelt by the puddle of blood, examined Benavente for a sign of life, then declared him dead.

"You could say I had mixed feelings about what happened," said the psychiatrist, Dr. Aub. "I hate sadists, I particularly hated what this one had done, and as I've already said, I didn't believe it was appropriate to say he was in any way a sick man. He deserved death if he deserved anything.

"But . . . I admit I had wanted a look at him. The analyst in me was interested, or maybe just nastily curious, to probe a little and find out what kind of stunted human spirit lay helpless behind his awfulness. The lawyer robbed me of that, so I was disappointed. Then again, the case ended on a note of retribution, so I had to be glad about that."

The third victim, the 16-year-old girl, was the step-daughter of the lawyer's sister. In a statement to a police officer, the lawyer admitted that he could hardly believe his luck when he was asked to stand as defence for the prisoner.

"I had felt murderous since that terrible thing was done to little Consuela," he said in his statement. "I had promised myself that one way or another, I would get close to the animal when they caught him, and somehow I would harm him. After I was appointed to defend him, it took a lot of restraint for me to leave the police station, go home and get my razor, then come back. All the time he was being charged, I wanted to let my control slip and just attack him with my bare hands, but I held back until I was equipped. I restrained myself because I felt he deserved the worst I could do."

There was a great tide of sympathy on the side of the lawyer. He was examined on behalf of the state by Dr. Aub, who declared him to be perfectly sane. The doctor added, however, that in his view, the inordinate emotional stress suffered by the lawyer, because of what had happened to the girl, had brought about a temporary imbalance of his mind. At the time he killed Manuel Benavente he had not been technically sane.

The court accepted that evaluation. The lawyer was asked to promise that he would undergo sixty weekly sessions of psychotherapy. He promised that he would and was immediately set free, with the judge's best wishes.

EIGHT

TRAVELLING MAN

At 6:00 am on a bright, cool Saturday morning in September 1994, the half-clothed body of a woman was found bundled under the bushes in a corner of the neatly landscaped Civic Centre Plaza in San Francisco. A police officer called to the scene shortly after the discovery described what he saw.

"She looked maybe twenty or so, very pretty, with long dark hair. Leaves and dirt were spread across her face and upper body. She had on a denim skirt and trainers, and a white sweater that was pulled up exposing her breasts. Her bra had been tied tightly around her neck. She had probably lain there all night, the body was very cold and her eyes had a milky film over them. The expression on her face was very serene, like somebody drowsing and just about to fall asleep. A female police officer joined me and a few moments later observed that the deceased's panties appeared to be missing."

The dead woman, 22-year-old Kay Uttley, had been a clerk at the San Francisco Advisory Centre. She lived with her mother and father in the small family hotel at Haight Ashbury, a ten-minute walk from her place of work. According to her mother, Kay had only ever had a few close friends, people she had known for years, and she never stepped outside that tight social circle. On the night she died, Kay had telephoned her mother to say she would be spending the evening with Patsy Lewis, one of her oldest friends from school.

"She told me not to wait up for her," Mrs. Uttley said. "She and Patsy were going to have dinner together and take in a late movie at the *Lumière* in the Civic Centre."

"As so often happens," said Detective Derek Voss of the San Francisco Police Department, "none of that story checked out. Patsy Lewis, an airline stewardess, wasn't even in town that night. Personnel at the *Lumière* were shown a picture of Kay Uttley but none of them recalled seeing her on the night in question. A check of bars and restaurants in the area pulled more blanks. One or two people recalled seeing Kay, but not recently."

While the autopsy got underway, Voss set up a team of experienced officers to work around the area of the Civic Centre and try to build a picture of Kay Uttley's movements on the night she died. Voss himself planned to interview Paul Chilton, Kay's immediate boss; a barman who had seen Kay a few times in recent weeks said she was with Chilton each time, and they appeared to be close.

"The barman knew Chilton because at one time he had commiserated with him about the various agonies surrounding his divorce," Voss said. "I saw the possibility of a scenario that could lead somewhere."

A few minutes before Voss left his office to call on Paul Chilton, a fax came in from the NYPD Crime Data Assembler.

"It's a department run by three women using these big computers linked to police information networks across the country," Voss explained. "The clever thing about the CDA is, it can draw comparisons at a speed that no human can come near, and it makes the comparisons on a scale of literally hundreds at one time. So if there are patterns to crime—inter-street, inter-town, or inter-state, CDA will detect them."

The fax informed Voss that forty-eight hours before the murder of Kay Uttley a superficially similar crime had been reported at Bodega Bay, 50 miles north of San Francisco.

"I put through a call to Bodega Bay and spoke to the police chief," Voss said. "He told me the case would probably be handled by one of our homicide teams here in San Francisco, since Bodega didn't have the facilities or the manpower, but meantime he could give me a rundown on the case. The victim was a 25-year-old local woman, Tessa Walden, whose body had been found in the woods north of the bay at Guerneville. The body was half-clothed when it was found. A skirt, sweater and shoes had been scattered in the bushes and the panties were missing, assuming she'd worn any. She had been strangled with her own bra."

Voss went to see Paul Chilton. He was a short, dapper man in his early forties who became noticeably nervous when Voss introduced himself.

"I didn't waste time on preliminaries," Voss said, "because now I was having doubts that this man had anything to do with Kay Uttley's death. The fax from CDA, plus what the chief at Bodega Bay told me, had started up that old feeling a homicide detective gets when certain facts come together. See, the two murders were relatively close geographically, and they were close in the way they had been committed. They were close to each other on the time scale, too. Now all that closeness—place, method, time—suggested that the same person committed both crimes. That likelihood raised another one, which was that the killer was not known to either woman.

"Now that's a headache for any homicide cop. If there's no relationship between victim and killer, then there is no limit on the range of potential suspects. Anybody could have committed those murders."

Paul Chilton denied there had been any closeness between him and Kay Uttley. They had got on well together, he said, but that was all. When Voss told him they had been seen out together drinking on more than one occasion, Chilton said it was often a good idea, when work overspilled the allotted time, to take business into a relaxing atmosphere somewhere and discuss it there.

"He believed it was good for staff relations," Voss said, "and he made out he was amazed that anybody would read anything else into his relationship with Miss Uttley. Well, I did for a start, and I got annoyed that he thought he could fob me off with that strictly-business front. He was a poor liar, and poor liars should have the sense to stick to the truth."

Voss told Chilton what he planned to do that afternoon. He was going to interview every member of staff in the office and find out if any of them believed there was more than a boss-employee relationship between Chilton and the murdered woman. Chilton told him to hang on, that wouldn't be necessary.

"When he told the truth, he wasn't half so obnoxious," Voss said. "He admitted that for a while he and Kay Uttley had been an item, though they had played it down, because she didn't want her parents to know she was seeing a man twenty years her senior, and she didn't want to upset her boyfriend, who was a student at the University of California medical centre. Kay wanted the social *status quo* to remain, he said, but she also wanted this thing that he and she had going. I asked him to elaborate on that. How come she wanted a relationship with him, but didn't want it to ruffle the lines of her life as it had been before?"

The relationship was purely sexual, Chilton said, blushing. Kay Uttley had a powerful sex drive that had been carefully suppressed through her teenage years, while she built up her safe and respectable little circle of friends and other social contacts. According to Chilton, she treated her sensual nature as a separate division of her personality, a set of characteristics segregated from everything she was determined to appear to be.

"She really liked the respectable, slightly staid, middle-class life," Chilton told Voss. "It was her ideal of a fulfilling existence. However, to be able to stay within those boundaries and to fit the mood of that life, she had to break out now and again."

Their first sexual encounter had happened a month after Chilton's divorce. He was feeling low in spirits and his self-esteem had taken a knock. So he asked Kay out to dinner. She hesitated at first and said she would let him know. He believed he had been gently rejected, but only an hour afterwards Kay said she would be happy to have dinner with him.

"It's the only time in my life I was sexually pressured. It started in the taxi on the way to the restaurant, it continued in little ways—touching feet, a hand on the knee under the tablecloth, not-so-coy innuendoes—right through dinner. I got so worked up I could hardly eat. I suggested we go back to my place, and she didn't resist. We went back and we had a really wild time, I'd never known anything like it. Afterwards, Kay told me she had always been highly sexed, but she knew it didn't fit with the kind of plans she had for herself."

Since the age of 15, Kay had taken occasional trips away from home, or sometimes just to other parts of the city, and she had deliberately picked up men for sex.

"I told her that was a very dangerous thing to do," Chilton said, "but she said she knew how to pick the right kind of man. She could always tell the type who would go along with her plans, but who wouldn't get out of control."

Chilton's relationship with Kay Uttley had ended, he confessed, when she had realised that he wanted more than sexual release with her. He was possessive by nature and Kay found the trait repellent. She ended the relationship, and for two months prior to her murder their association had been strictly professional.

"I believed him," Voss said. "Anybody would. When his guard was down he was transparent. I left the office feeling kind of sorry for him."

The autopsy on Kay Uttley revealed that, as suspected, she had died of strangulation. Shortly before she died she had engaged in sex and a quantity of semen was retrieved. The autopsy on the other dead woman, Tessa Walden, revealed that she too had been strangled, and like Kay she had had sexual intercourse close to the time of death.

"It had been noted early in the investigation," Voss said, "that the knot used to tie the bra around the victim's neck, in each case, was identical. So there was no doubt at all that the same man committed both murders. We fully expected to get a lead on the killer's blood group, too, when the semen test results came back, but we were out of luck. The lab told us the murderer hadn't been a so-called secretor. That meant he wasn't one of the 80 per cent of the population who transmit blood-group antigens in their sweat, saliva and semen."

Later, Voss was told by his departmental administrators that his homicide team was being temporarily enlarged, so that he could incorporate the murder of Tessa Walden into his investigation.

"It was more work but it made sense," Voss said. "I got together all the notes that had been compiled on Tessa and I discovered she had some characteristics in common with Kay Uttley, although she had been less discreet than Kay. Tessa had been known to like the company of men more than women, she had had a couple of affairs in her home territory that had gone public when the wives got to know about it, and there was even a porno video, produced by a New York company, in which Tessa featured prominently. She had told friends she was recruited for the one-off job by a customer in a diner where she had worked, and she did it because the money was good and she got to screw some good-looking guys."

It would have been easy, Voss said, to go ahead and draw high-flying conclusions from the fact that both murdered women had embraced sexual activity with more than average enthusiasm. The significant fact, probably, was that they were not difficult to approach.

"A guy with the right approach and appearance wouldn't encounter much resistance from either of them," Voss said. "I'd been a homicide detective long enough to know that a big percentage of female murder victims were friendly girls who liked a few laughs and appreciative company. They were sitting targets for psychos."

Four days after the murder of Kay Uttley, another woman was found murdered, this time in the Japanese Tea Garden in the Golden Gate Park.

"Same MO as before," Voss said. "The body was half-clothed, the underpants were missing, and she had been strangled with her bra, which was tied the same way as the other two. This time the victim was a 20-year-old nurse, Susan Gazeley, who hadn't shown up for duty the previous evening. It didn't take long to establish that Susan had been a friendly, outgoing girl with an impressively long sexual history for someone her age."

The police were now officially looking for a multiple-victim killer; the term "serial killer" was gradually being abandoned in favour of a catch-all description. Serial killers were taken to be people who committed several murders, singly, over a period; mass murderers, on the other hand, killed many people at the same time. An umbrella term, it was felt, saved misunderstanding, and could always be qualified by a description of the crimes in question.

"Try as we might," Voss said, "we couldn't find any witnesses who saw Tessa, Kay, or Susan with a man on the dates they were murdered. In fact we didn't find anyone at all who had seen any of the three women close to the times they died. As matters stood, we didn't have anything to go on. I foresaw the catalogue of murders starting to grow, but I tried not to think of us spending months and months getting nowhere."

The first useful clue was provided by Terry Daffin, a forensic biologist on attachment from Harvard University to the University of California. He had been shown the case notes on the three murdered women by an acquaintance in the Medical Examiner's Department, and he recognised the killer's *modus operandi*. He remembered the expression of hope that seemed to light up Voss's face as he told him what he knew.

"The sliding and locking knot used to cause strangulation had first been noticed in a murder at public swimming baths in Denver, Colorado, five years before," Daffin said. "I was helping out on a separate enquiry at the time but I sat in on the strangulation as well. The victim was a waitress from the cafeteria up on the second floor at the swimming baths. In her break time she had been seen talking to a sharply-dressed young man out on the lawn behind the building. Two hours later she was dead in the bushes, strangled not with her bra, but her apron. The knot, however, was exactly the same one used in the three San Francisco murders."

Daffin had already contacted the Denver Police Forensic Investigation Department, and the details of that earlier case had been faxed to him. The killer of the waitress had been caught on eyewitness evidence, and on a number of forensic clues, including fibres from her clothes on his jacket, and a deposit of her saliva on the cuff of an unwashed shirt taken from his hotel.

"The killer's name was Dennis Reeve," Daffin said. "He had been sent to prison for the murder of the waitress, but the record showed that he had been released a month prior to the first of the San Francisco killings. His parole officer in Colorado reported that Reeve had vanished and had taken every scrap of his belongings with him.

"He was a complex character," Daffin recalled. "He had a university education and for a time he worked as a junior lecturer at an engineering school. Then there was some trouble with a woman—she said he'd tried to strangle her during sex—and he gave up teaching. Gave up pretty well everything, it seemed. He worked for a couple of weeks at a time to make enough money to move around freely for a month. He was a travelling man, always roaming, never in the same place for long. That was how he lived up till the time he killed the waitress."

A photograph of Dennis Reeve was circulated to police officers and the staff of public buildings. Anyone having any information at all was to get in touch with Derek Voss or a member of his team. On the same day the picture was circulated, the manager of a car hire company came to the police station and asked to speak to Voss.

"He was really excited," Voss said. "He tapped the big picture of Reeve we had hanging on the wall and he said, 'That's him, that guy, that's him, the one that hired a car off me twelve days ago.' "

The car had been rented for an initial period of seven days, but it had never been returned.

"We put out a description of the car," Voss said, "and an hour later a couple of cops patrolling around Union Square found it tucked into an alley. We had it towed in and I asked Terry Daffin if he would like to give it the expert's once over."

Daffin said he would love to. He asked if he could bring along two assistants and some specialised equipment. Voss said he could bring along whoever and whatever he wanted.

"I wasn't being so carelessly generous as people might have thought. In the short time since we'd been acquainted I had been hearing amazing things about Terry Daffin. At the University of California they reckoned he was the finest forensic investigator they'd had on the faculty—from both a teaching and a practical point of view. So I wasn't letting some dummy loose on the car; I was sending in the best person for the job."

Daffin, for his part, was determined to make a case and make it stick. While he was confident he could do that, he was slightly nervous of the amount of faith Voss placed in him.

"There's a presumption that because I work with DNA in my investigative work, I'm somehow in possession of the key to all mysteries, and if a case comes under my scrutiny, then it's bound to get solved; but the facts are very different. Working with DNA as a tool of identification is a revolutionary way to get at the truth of many criminal acts, but it's also infuriatingly tricky and unpredictable."

One lesson a scientist learns quickly in his work with DNA material is that it is unstable. It corrupts very easily. Swabs taken from nasal passages, mouths, vaginas and anuses have to be air dried as soon as possible, and they must not be subjected to heat. If there is any likelihood of a delay in sending them to the laboratory, they have to be stored in a deep freeze. Semen in rape cases has to be taken from the victim's body in a pipette, put in a small test tube and frozen solid as fast as possible if there is to be any hope of obtaining useful DNA material from it at the laboratory.

"There's a lot of mythology surrounding human hair," Daffin said. "Many people believe that when you have a human hair in your possession, you have a potential blueprint of that person. A hair, whatever part of the body it comes from, is useless for human profiling unless there's a great enough number of root or follicle cells attached to the bulb.

"Body organs—that's another area of huge misunderstanding. Even if you've got a whole organ to work with, you can only use certain parts, and they have to be in good, decay-free condition. The couple of grams of material you need have to come from the parenchyma of the organ—that's the functioning part, as distinct from the framework. The tissue has to go into a plastic tube with no fixative and no preservative, and it has to be frozen solid as fast as you can do it."

In spite of all his avowed reservations about the use of DNA in investigative work, few people know more about it than Terry Daffin, and in the examination of the car used by the suspected killer, Dennis Reeve, he brought all his considerable skill to bear.

"I naturally thought he would search the car for traces of Dennis Reeve," Voss said, "and indeed he did that, although as he pointed out afterwards, until such time as we had a hold of Reeve, there was no telling whose traces had been collected from the car. However, all the time, at the forefront of Daffin's mind, there had been the hope of finding something else."

Forty-eight hours after exhaustively searching the car, after swabbing, lifting with tape, photographing, dusting, collecting with forceps and plastic bags and, finally, filter-vacuuming the entire interior, Daffin said he had found something very significant.

"It's a hair," he said.

Voss said he did his best to look encouraged. A single hair, complete with root bulb, had been found in the front of the car, and DNA material derived from it had been subjected to careful analysis.

"I didn't know what was the right thing to say," Voss admitted. "At that moment, it appeared that all the other material taken from the car had been discounted."

To analyse the DNA from the hair, Daffin had used a highly advanced technique which is now regarded as one of the great hopes for the future of DNA profiling. The technique is called polymerase chain reaction—PCR. DNA polymerase makes the bonds of phosphate in the "back-bone" of the DNA double helix. In the PCR technique, the DNA is chemically encouraged by the polymerase to replicate itself. The outcome is that a small amount of genetic material turns into a large amount. In practical terms, this means that the DNA in a small sample—so small it cannot be used for profiling—can be used to reproduce enough of itself to make testing possible.

"The DNA from that single hair produced an elegant profile," Daffin said. "To be precise, it gave me a chemical profile of Reeve's third victim in San Francisco, Susan Gazeley."

So Susan Gazeley had been in Reeve's hired car. That fact alone was enough to sustain a powerful case. Over the following days, dust consistent with that on the soles of Kay Uttley's trainers was found, as well as cosmetic powder traces identical in composition to a make-up base worn by Tessa Walden.

"The hard part was over," Voss said. "We knew who the killer was, all we had to do was find him. I'd like to say that astute police work tracked him down, but it didn't. He travelled right across the country before an alert airport detective spotted him checking in for a flight at LaGuardia in New York."

Dennis Reeve denied all knowledge of any crime, and continued to deny his involvement throughout the time he was in custody. By the time he was formally charged with the murders of Tessa Walden, Kay Uttley and Susan Gazeley, the scientific evidence against him was overwhelming. Terry Daffin, backed by the

resources of the University of California, had produced a lucid, richly detailed dossier of scientific
proofs which demonstrated Reeve's guilt.

"Three days before Reeve was due to appear in
court for the start of his trial," Voss said, "he hanged
himself in his police cell. He hanged himself but he
didn't die, because after half a minute or so, the pipe
to which he'd attached the purloined length of string
broke away from the ceiling. He wound up with a
sprained ankle and a really sore throat.

"The amusing part, though, was the way that Terry
Daffin wouldn't pass up anything that was construc-
tively evidential. By the time the prosecution evidence
was being unfurled before the mesmerised jury, it
contained the information that not only were the knots
tied in the three victims' bras identical, but they
matched the knot in the twine with which Dennis
Reeve tried to hang himself in the cell."

During the trial Dennis Reeve showed signs of extreme mental imbalance. Two psychiatrists attested to
the fact that he was acutely and incurably psychotic.
They added that he would constitute a serious risk to
public safety if he were ever allowed to go free.

The eventual sentence of the court was that Reeve
be sent to a secure facility for the criminally insane,
where he should remain for the duration of his life.

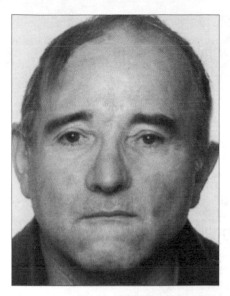

A Dream of Power: Federico Bascos, multiple murderer who killed women with "aphrodisiac" drinks.

Jorge Perlosio, Spanish authority on poisons and poisoning.

Penfriend: Detective Luciano Lattes, on the track of a killer who specialised in castrating sexual offenders.

Dr. Domenico Fortini: he stretched the limits of scientific detection to pinpoint the murderer.

Ego Tripper:

1. Bullet hole in the jacket of Morton Conroy; some scorching is visible.

2. The same bullet hole photographed by infra-red, showing the pressure contour of the weapon.

3. Muzzle of the pistol found in the property of Harriet Mason, clearly identifiable as the weapon used to shoot Conroy.

4. Bullet hole in Conroy's chest—but no bullet was found in the body.

5. The key-gripper forceps used by Harriet Mason.

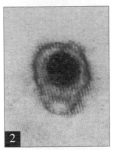

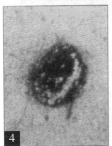

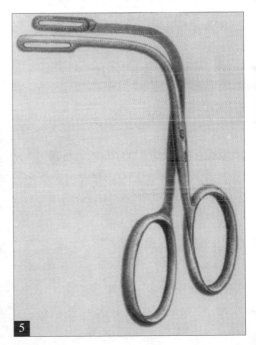

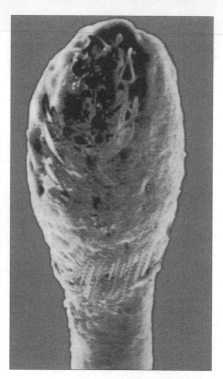

Travelling Man:
A photomicrograph of the hair root which revealed a DNA profile of Susan Gazely. It also proved she had been in Dennis Reeve's car.

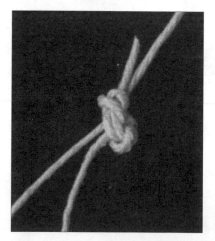

The knot in the twine with which Reeve tried to hang himself in prison. It was identical to the knots tied in all three murder victims' bras.

Stalker: Chemical disclosure of one of the "dead" man's prints on the second threatening note.

Dr. Sherman Fields, whose forensic detective work finally led to the arrest of Allan Crowder.

IS THAT CHILD REALLY YOURS?

IT'S EASY TO FIND OUT.

BLOOD GROUPING DOES NOT LIE!

matings	possible offspring	impossible offspring
O X O	O	A, B, AB
O X A	O, A	B, AB
O X B	O, B	A, AB
O X AB	A, B	O, AB
A X A	O, A	B, AB
A X B	O, A, B, AB	
A X AB	A, B, AB	O
B X B	O, B	A, AB
B X AB	A, B, AB	O
AB X AB	A, B, AB	O

Bad Blood: The "paternity table," cut from a magazine, that helped turn Sidney Loomis into a killer.

Pyro: The remote house where Mia Clark lived alone.

Mia Clark at the time of her arrest.

One of Nick Lubbock's speculative drawings of the device Mia used to burn down four retirement homes and kill 60 people.

Hypostasis: The appearance of a body that has lain on its right side. The arrow indicates an area of normal skin colour where blood has not been allowed to drain.

NINE

STALKER

In the late 1960s and throughout the 1970s, Harry Crowder was a popular American television actor, performing guest roles in a number of sitcoms and domestic dramas. In 1974 he landed his own series, a gentle family comedy based around a widowed lawyer bringing up his three children single-handedly in a rural mid-western town. The series was an immediate hit which ran for an entire decade. In 1984, having carefully banked and invested his money during his twenty successful years in television, Crowder bought a mansion among the homes of the movie stars at Bel Air. On the day he moved in, he called a press conference and announced his retirement from acting.

"I'm 60, I've had a good career, I've done all the things I wanted to do in television, and I'm not short of a buck or two. So it's time for me to lie back and soak up the California sunshine."

The mansion was vast. For a man living alone— Crowder had a personal assistant, Audrey Neal, who went home at night; two gardeners who worked mornings only; a night-duty security guard and a boxer dog—the place seemed ridiculously large.

The house formed a square around a central courtyard with a large ornamental fountain, a ceramic copy of an original in the Citadel Park in Mexico City. On the ground floor were three reception rooms, a long sitting room with a fitted bar at each end, a dining room, a drawing room, a library and a games room. Upstairs there were six bedrooms with adjoining bathrooms, a sun lounge and a small cinema. The basement housed a sauna, a gym and an extensive laundry facility. The lawns and gardens covered an acre of landscaped hillside; to the rear of a reproduction Castilian greenhouse, where Crowder planned to grow exotic fruit, there was a ten-foot wall surrounding an Olympic-size swimming pool.

"Harry Crowder was really happy there for about a month," said the PA, Audrey Neal. At the time Crowder moved into the mansion she was 29, a strikingly attractive blonde, and she knew people were saying that she was really his mistress. "I could handle that. I was a trained secretary and there had been rumours about me and all three of the businessmen I had worked for in the years since I left college. That was OK, there's always some kind of price to pay for having a good job *and* good looks. People automatically think I'm an airhead with a trick pelvis and no scruples to get in the way of my ambition."

The fact was that Audrey believed in keeping her job and her private life separated. She found the rumours surrounding her and Harry Crowder particularly amusing because Crowder was a celibate homosexual.

"Five days a week I attended to his fan mail and all his regular correspondence, which amounted to quite a bundle. I kept the household accounts in order, kept the various cupboards stocked, ordered the gardeners around, walked the dog, and organised the little weekly get-togethers Harry threw for friends and neighbours. The announcement he made to the press when he retired was the whole truth—he planned to relax, sun himself, and generally let the remainder of his life be one nice long vacation."

Five weeks after Crowder moved into the mansion, he began receiving ominous notes in his mailbox. The first one, postmarked Hollywood, was typewritten on blue paper and read:

YOU DON'T DESERVE THE LIFE YOU'VE CHOSEN.
I WILL MAKE IT TURN BAD ON YOU.

There was no signature, and Crowder pretended to dismiss the note as the work of a harmless crank.

"But it got to him, all right," Audrey said. "He was a sensitive man, he had always shied away from reading bad reviews, not that he ever had many. The only kind of mail he got from the public, year in and year out, was the gushing flattering kind. He was tuned to niceness, he couldn't cope with anything nasty."

The second note came three days after the first, postmarked Hollywood as before. The address was typed but the note was written in pencil, in big capital letters on the same blue paper:

> WATCH FOR ME, HARRY. I'M WATCHING
> YOU, WAITING TO HURT YOU. AQUARIUS
> CAN DO THAT.

"I wanted to take the notes to the police," Audrey said, "but Harry didn't want that. He didn't want any ripples across his peace, and he especially didn't want armed guards patrolling the gardens and standing at the gate, like some of the neighbours had. His retirement meant freedom to him, a kind of release, because what the public never knew was that Harry hated acting, he hated television and everything connected with it. He had served his time, he told me. He wasn't going back to the trapped life for anybody."

Crowder started watching the gates from an upstairs window. He used a long-range telescope, and occasionally when he was walking in the gardens he would carry binoculars, and he would scan the perimeter wall several times, trying to look casual about it, as if he were simply surveying his property.

"He was scared somebody would get in," Audrey said. "There were cameras on the walls, on the gates and all round the outside of the house, but because the threat was so vague, it left room for imagination, and Harry's ran wild. He would be talking about something like a new ice cream he had discovered, or the way he was going to re-arrange the furniture in the sitting room, and all at once he would stop and stand up and peer through his binoculars. At other times he told me how ridiculous it was that anybody would pick on him, threaten him, because he hadn't made an enemy in his life. He was really frightened."

The third note came two days after the second. Audrey could see the fear on Crowder's face as he unfolded the blue paper. It said:

TODAY, HARRY, TODAY IT BEGINS. AQUARIUS
HAS THE POWER.

"He began to crack up," Audrey said. "I don't think I ever saw a guy so sensitive. He held out the note to me, opened his mouth to say something but just sort of shuddered instead and gulped like he was swallowing something enormous. On impulse I put my arms around him as if he was a child, and he let me. I told him not to get this thing out of proportion, it was what he'd said it was in the first place, crank mail. The stars get it all the time, they handle it, they take precautions and they put up barriers between themselves and the people who want to frighten them or hurt them."

Harry Crowder looked ill for the rest of that day. In the afternoon he told Audrey that all his life he had carried at the back of his mind the thought that, if he ever found happiness, someone would come along and take it all away from him. A fortune teller in Santa Monica had told him, forty years before, that he would eventually be a victim of something "nameless and dark" if he didn't protect himself. "But she never told me how," he said.

Audrey realised for the first time how superstitious he was. "Those Aquarius references, they were aimed right at something vulnerable in his psyche. I quizzed him about it."

Crowder said he didn't know what the remarks about Aquarius meant. Audrey didn't believe him. To make it easier for him to talk about it, she suggested it could be something he had suppressed, and that if he thought about it calmly he would remember. He insisted, again, that he didn't know what the references meant, he had never known what they meant, and he had suppressed nothing. Audrey tried a little harder, then drew back, realising that the intensity of her questioning was putting her near the point where she might find herself without a job.

"He was getting mad at me," Audrey said. "So I apologised; I said I was just trying to find a way to help. He accepted that and I think he forgave me for being so pushy."

That evening Harry Crowder followed his usual bedtime practice of spraying his nasal passages with a decongestant prescribed by his doctor. Except this time it wasn't his medication he sprayed into his nose, but something that burned like fire. Screaming with pain he ran out of the house to the security booth by the gate. The guard called the emergency medical service and tried to calm his boss. Crowder was in terrible pain. He kept yelling at the guard to hurry it up and running outside to splash water in his face from a drinking fountain.

The paramedics eventually came, and after a quick examination of Crowder's nose they decided he would have to be treated in hospital. They took him to the emergency room where a technician took away the nasal spray for examination while a doctor treated Crowder for severe irritation of the nasal passages and upper facial sinuses.

"The laboratory technician took it on himself to call the police," Audrey said. "Harry was mad about that, but it had happened and he couldn't undo it. Besides, it was obvious now that something positive had to be done. He had to fight back at whoever was out to harm him. The spray contained a dilute solution of acetic acid, strong enough to cause serious dehydration and burning. A surgeon told Harry that bad as it was, it could have been much worse."

The police took charge of the nasal spray. The detective in charge of the investigation, Bud Altman of the LAPD, asked Audrey if she knew the significance of the label on the bottom of the bottle. Audrey looked. It was the Zodiac symbol for Aquarius.

Crowder's recovery took a long time. The delicate membranes of the nose, sinuses and upper throat had all been severely damaged. It caused him serious pain to swallow, and he could only take liquid nourishment, administered through a tube that bypassed the slowly healing tissues.

"I couldn't get much of a handle on what was happening," Detective Altman said. "Mr. Crowder didn't want to communicate. I would have pressed harder if he had been in better shape, and if I'd believed he was protecting somebody; but he was really sick, and I could tell he was as much in the dark as the rest of us. I decided to wait, just snoop around in his background for a while, and later maybe lean on him a little harder to come up with a name or two, and perhaps a beginning of a theory about how an intruder got into the house and tampered with his medication."

Around this time Audrey Neal put herself on voluntary suspension and waived her salary for the time she would be away. "It was important I be ruled out as a suspect as soon as I could," she said. "No one was closer to Harry, so naturally I had to be in the frame from the police point of view—maybe from Harry's, too."

Security at the mansion was now round the clock, and the usual one-man guard was swollen to six during the day and four at night. Heat-sensing alarms were installed and the boxer now had three highly disciplined Dobermanns for company.

The fourth note arrived ten days after the third, with the midday mail. That morning, Harry Crowder had been upstairs with his binoculars and he saw a woman standing across the road from the main gate, staring at the house. She was dressed all in black, with a wide-brimmed hat and a black veil covering the lower half of her face. He called Detective Altman, who drove straight over to the mansion. By that time, the woman had disappeared.

"It sounded like pure theatre to me," Altman said, "but it scared the living bejesus out of Crowder. To hear him tell it, you'd think he'd seen the reaper. He was halfway out of himself, gulping and waving his arms, and I thought, somebody knows how to scare this guy without a lot of effort."

Altman was still at the mansion when the note arrived. Crowder recognised the envelope, so Altman told him to hand it over; he would open it wearing latex gloves. The note was on the same paper as the other two:

ARE YOU OVER YOUR SNIFFLES, HARRY?
WORSE IS ON THE WAY. AQUARIUS CAN REACH
YOUR HEART.

"The note itself was enough to set him juddering," Altman said, "even if he didn't know what it meant. I did what I could to reassure him. I reminded him the place was heavily guarded night and day, and that he was only ever a button-press away from immediate help. That didn't pacify him much. The fear had gotten inside his head and, because he couldn't define it, the presence was very potent, like a malignant ghost."

Next afternoon, Crowder put through an urgent call to his doctor and another to Detective Altman. The doctor, Lloyd Rainer, got there first and found Crowder in a state close to collapse.

"I examined him and found his blood pressure was

markedly raised," Rainer said. "He was fatigued, he complained of a sense of fullness in the neck and the abdomen, and his ankles were swollen. These signs suggested to me that Harry was suffering from right-ventricular heart failure."

Right-ventricular or right-sided heart failure is a condition resulting from failure of the heart to main-tain adequate circulation of the blood, due to inade-quate output by the right ventricle.

"It can arise from a number of causes," Rainer said. "Arteriosclerosis, pericarditis, coronary disease—I was surprised that I hadn't spotted some symptoms before, but there it was, the signs were clear and un-mistakable."

Crowder's reaction to the provisional diagnosis was to start panicking.

"It's what he said!" he yelled. "Aquarius can reach my heart! Jesus Christ he's doing it! He's doing it!"

Crowder grew so distressed that Dr. Rainer had to sedate him. In the meantime Detective Altman col-lated the background information on Crowder and tried to construct a line of enquiry.

"I was used to compiling criminal histories," Alt-man said. "This was completely different. I had a rec-ord of Harry Crowder's career from the first time he set foot in a TV studio right up to the time he retired, at the close of filming on the sixth season of his sit-com. It was the chronicle of a career in entertainment, and it read like a name-dropper's prompt sheet, but I have to say, for a showbiz life it was pretty free of scandal."

Crowder had lived in Los Angeles with his parents and his younger brother, Alan, until he was 20. At that time, having landed a contract to do "background" work in films and television programmes, he was earning enough money to support himself, and he moved into a small apartment off Hollywood Boulevard. From then until his retirement he rented a succession of apartments and bungalows, some of which he shared with lovers, though none of his relationships with other men appeared to last for very long.

"Naturally, I was hoping to find a clue in his background," Altman said, "a former partner with a grudge, something of the kind, but there was no record of that, no hint in the files or the press clippings to suggest acrimony or a feud between Crowder and anyone he had known. It wasn't that he was a goodie-goodie, he was just cautious; he never hung out with people with a higher speed rating than he had."

A former lover revealed that Crowder had been celibate since 1981 when rumours of a "gay plague" were circulating in the Hollywood area, and reports of the Homosexual Compromise Syndrome, later to be called AIDS, were appearing in the scientific and medical literature.

"He had no enemies at all, as far as I could tell," Crowder's former agent said. "But he had no close friends, either. Gradually, as time went by and he dropped his membership from this and that club and organisation, I realised that his isolation—that's what it amounted to—was based on his canny handling of money. He was not a man who believed in letting anything encroach on his capital. Even the extravagant mansion and the weekly parties, all that was paid for out of profit. He was a big-time no-risk investor who never wasted a dollar in his life. People like that rarely have any real friends. I think it's because their order of priorities puts relationships at a position some way down the scale from investment husbandry and fiscal management in general."

Dr. Rainer put Crowder on drug therapy for his apparent heart condition. "We ran all the tests first, of course," Rainer said, "and although they confirmed the picture of RV heart failure, they were *not* a classic indication of the condition. It was hard to say what wasn't right—maybe it was in the relative severity of one symptom compared to another, the way they didn't contrast the way we would have expected. To this day I can't pinpoint it. I just know we were sure he had RV heart failure, even though we found the test results kind of unusual."

Three nurses worked eight-hour shifts at Crowder's mansion to monitor his condition and make sure he rested and took his medicine at the correct times. But he did not seem to respond to the medication: if anything his condition became slightly worse. On the fourth day of treatment he had an attack of palpitations that lasted an hour and left him terrified. When the nurse on duty had calmed him and Dr. Rainer came and administered a sedative, Crowder asked to speak to Detective Altman.

"He told me he was totally in the dark, but just the same, he had to tell somebody the little bit he'd held back. He said that for all he knew, his life depended on him revealing what the Aquarius stuff meant.

"Harry Crowder himself was Capricorn. His younger brother Alan was the one called Aquarius. Those were their birth signs and from the time Harry was 12 and his brother was 9, they called each other by those names. The idea was Alan's; he was heavily into astrology. When Harry left home at the age of 20, Alan wanted to go with him. He didn't want to go on living in the house with the parents, not without his brother there—Harry said that Alan believed his older brother was his best friend. Harry, however, didn't want Alan tagging along; he didn't want any adhesions from the life he was leaving for good. This was his threshold time, the first step into the arena of his future. The last thing he wanted was his kind of whiny, kind of creepy kid brother hanging around like some depressing reminder of his mediocre roots.

"Alan took the rejection badly. Some time after Harry left home Alan did too, but he wasn't stepping on a ladder that pointed up. According to Harry, it was a chute that went straight down. Alan went to live in a commune with a herd of dropouts and pretty soon he was in trouble with the law."

Detective Altman had already checked the rap sheet: Alan Crowder had arrests for possession of drugs, for being drunk and disorderly, and for lewd behaviour with a female minor.

"He had also been apprehended while impersonating a female in the commission of a hold-up at a mini-mart," Altman said. "But in legal terms all that was a closed book, because in 1973 Alan had died in a house fire that claimed the lives of three other dropouts. In superstitious terms, though, Alan's death was not so much an ending as a new beginning. Harry Crowder was prepared to believe that his dead brother was reaching out to him from beyond and doing him dirt."

Apart from the coldness that grew between the brothers when Harry left home, Harry had alienated his brother later, and much more severely, by refusing him any financial help in 1970, when Alan was being hounded by street loan sharks who were owed $2,000 and threatened broken legs if Alan didn't pay up. In the end, Alan raised the money from a drugstore heist, for which he was never arrested, although the police knew that he and two of his friends carried out the robbery.

"Harry was convinced that was what it was all about. Somehow his brother, dead and gone, was in touch again, and getting his own back by torturing Harry's nerves and killing him off a piece at a time."

Around this time Detective Altman had mentioned the odd aspects of the Crowder case to Dr. Sherman Fields, a forensic medical specialist with the LAPD.

"I was fascinated straight away," Fields said. "I think it was the mention of Crowder's sudden and unexpected illness. I was familiar with one or two conditions that mimicked heart failure, and naturally, given the nature of my job, and the fact that there were so-called supernatural overtones to the case, I was deeply suspicious."

Sherman Fields spoke to Dr. Rainer and asked if he would mind a cynical forensic man taking a look at his patient. Rainer said he would be intrigued to know of any new slant on the case.

"I think Harry Crowder mistrusted me, at the beginning," Fields said. "I was young, perhaps a little brash, and he was a frightened man who saw anything new or unexplained, at that time, as profoundly threatening. I talked with him, I was patient, I made myself shut up and listen to his tentative inching-out of his neurotic terror. By and by he saw I was a serious individual, and I think he caught on to my genuine interest in what was making him ill. Quite soon he relaxed and started getting receptive to what I said."

Fields asked Crowder if he had ever suffered a serious allergy as a child or a young adult, anything that might produce physical symptoms such as a rash or swelling. Crowder said he believed that his mother had been warned that he shouldn't eat certain things— mostly to do with confectionery, as far as he could recall.

"He told me he got round that by giving up candy when he was still in his teens. He hadn't touched it since. Except, he said, for the chewing gum."

The chewing gum had first been taken to substitute for cigarettes when he gave up smoking in 1969. He had been hooked on gum ever since and chewed his way through two packets a day. He kept a variety of different types on hand and liked switching brands from day to day.

"One of my theories about his heart failure leapt to

the fore," Fields said. "I got back to Dr. Rainer and asked him to look back in Crowder's record and see if there was any mention of a sensitivity to liquorice. He did as I asked, and bingo, there it was, more than forty years before: a clear note on the record saying Harry Crowder was acutely sensitive to the effects of glycyrrhizinic acid—a component of liquorice."

Anyone with a sensitivity to liquorice was likely to suffer from heightened blood pressure, a recurring sense of abdominal fullness, and swollen ankles. Fields went back to Crowder's mansion and asked Harry to show him the stockpile of chewing gum.

"He had a little cupboard in the kitchen full of the stuff. It was in every imaginable flavour, and seemed to have come from all over the world. When I asked him where he bought it, he said he didn't. He simply left an order with a downtown store to supply him with the stuff, and he paid the bill once a month. 'I eat any kind of gum,' he told me, 'so I don't care about brand or flavour or whatever. Variety. That's all I ask.' "

Fields took away one packet of each different kind of chewing gum and passed them to the analytical chemists at the LAPD Forensic Science Laboratory.

"Bingo again," he said. "Every one of those packets of gum contained liquorice in one form or another."

A check was made with the store which supplied the gum. The manager said that a few weeks ago, a young woman had come in and said that in future Mr. Crowder would like only the brands and flavours of chewing gum specified on a typed list she gave the clerk. The list was on Mr. Crowder's headed note-paper, so the manager didn't hesitate to implement the request.

"I explained this to Crowder, how someone had deliberately changed his chewing gum order so he would only have gum that contained liquorice. He was nervous and mystified at the notion of some woman knowing so much about him and going to such lengths to do him harm. On the other hand, he was relieved that his heart failure was probably spurious and nothing more than an allergic reaction."

Fields realised that there was more work to be done yet before Crowder's condition could be alleviated. "Chewing gum alone would not have made him ill. He was bound to have eaten gum containing liquorice before, and probably the small amounts absorbed that way were not enough, in themselves, to set off a full-blown reaction. If my theory was correct, there had to be some other source of liquorice in Crowder's daily diet. I reckoned somebody was packing the stuff into him any way they could, just to get the symptoms up and running."

Fields made a thorough search of the kitchen and was astonished at the thoroughness of Harry Crowder's tormentor.

"There was liquorice everywhere," he said. "It was in his herbal tea, in the ground coffee, the pepper grinder, the herb jars. It was in the bottles of vinai-grette and most of the other dressings. It had been added to the strong-flavoured MultiVeg drink Harry took every morning. His intake of liquorice, one way and another, was well above average, when of course it should have been way below average—in fact he shouldn't have been taking any at all."

As soon as the liquorice was removed from Crowder's diet, his symptoms disappeared—but the mystery remained. Who had done this to him, and how had they managed it?

Dr. Fields and Detective Altman sat down to talk over the case. It was clear to both of them that an insider was at work, even though there were no obvious culprits. Altman admitted he would like to have a forensic slant on the case, since the police approach had so far led nowhere.

Fields asked if any fingerprints had been found on the notes. Altman said no—there was something there, especially on the last note received, but the lab couldn't get a print to develop.

"I was brash enough to shove my nose into the fingerprint experts' domain and make a suggestion," Fields said. "A lot of my early training was with a couple of forensic general practitioners, which is to say they did everything—medical, fibres, fingerprints, all the branches—and they taught me some heroic techniques for getting results from what they called reticent evidence—that's evidence not willing to yield up its little secrets."

The chemical treatment of documents is not encouraged if the documents themselves are likely to be crucial to a prosecution case. Chemical tests often damage valuable evidence, and in cases where electrostatic testing might be necessary at some stage, prior chemical treatment of any kind destroys a document's potential for this kind of examination.

"But there are times when chemical tests offer the only hope of finding latent fingerprints," Fields said, "and in those cases, certain fingerprint experts apply the ninhydrin test. It's the way I was taught. The technique doesn't always work, but when it does the results are impressively clear."

Documents to be tested are floated on a solution of triketohydrindene hydrate—short name, ninhydrin—and gently rocked to and fro, in the same way that a photographic print is developed. After a short time, if latent fingerprints exist in any strength, they will show up as dark images.

"The method has brought up prints on envelopes, bank-notes and even subway tickets," Fields said. "I pointed out that there were three notes in the case, so one could surely be risked on the ninhydrin technique. It wasn't as if it would be destroyed, I said, and there was always the chance we'd get a print and maybe get the case moving."

The ninhydrin test produced two clear thumbprints.

"We submitted them to the national print database. They found a match, and it was quite a surprise. According to records, the prints belonged to a man who had been dead for eleven years."

The dead man was Alan Crowder, Harry Crowder's young brother. Police and forensic workers were dumbfounded. Apart from the supernatural implications of the finding—which might have sent Harry Crowder insane had he been told—there was the possibility that a disastrous flaw existed in the national fingerprint database. Calm consideration prevailed, however, and Fields and Altman soon figured out what had happened.

"Nothing new, really, but nothing too common, either," Fields said. "One of the bodies in the fire was wearing neck-tag ID and a bracelet that identified it as the remains of Alan Crowder, but it couldn't have been him. Whether by accident or design, Alan had got himself registered non-existent, which probably solved a lot of problems at one stroke. Now, the years had passed, and he was deciding, for whatever reason, to visit some payback on his big brother."

By this time Harry Crowder, who knew nothing about the fingerprint breakthrough, had decided that the mysterious woman he had seen standing opposite the mansion gate was behind the things that were being done to him. For the time being Detective Altman decided to let him go on thinking that.

"The time to tell him," Altman said, "would be when we collared the brother and were in a position to resurrect him right in front of Harry."

A fingerprint search of the mansion showed that Alan Crowder had recently been in the kitchen. The worktops were wiped down regularly, but his prints were found in eight separate areas.

"I began to feel like a jerk," Altman said. "It was obvious that in a household of so few people, the culprit had to be right under our noses. We were agreed it had to be one of the two gardeners. So we pulled them in and fingerprinted them."

The gardeners, however, were above suspicion.

"They were painfully honest men," Fields said. "No criminal records, spotless references—I felt sorry for Altman, the way he had to apologise to them. They were really upset that anybody could think they were dishonest, and I think it was embarrassed reaction and frustration that made Detective Altman turn on me."

"That's what I did," Altman agreed, "I turned on Dr. Fields, I accused him of sticking his nose in too far and for too long, and I asked him what in hell a medical forensic specialist was doing tagging along with an investigation of this kind, anyway. I simmered down and apologised right away, but he answered my question anyway. He said the case was a nice break from the endless daily business of looking at dead bodies and determining a cause of death. He said it was also confirming him in the belief that he was truly a general forensic man at heart, not a specialist. He also said it was now his turn to apologise."

Altman didn't see why Dr. Fields should apologise for anything. A further explanation cleared up the point.

"I told him I had been conducting an investigation of my own," Fields said. "When the fingerprint check had shown that the gardeners were in the clear, I called up the estate management outfit that dealt with most of the grounds and garden staff employed around Bel Air. I told them I was with the LAPD, which strictly speaking was true. I asked if one of the gardeners at Mr. Crowder's place had recently been changed. They checked and the answer was yes. It wasn't unusual, all their men were screened, one was as reliable as another. I asked if they could tell me where the gardener had gone. A minute later they had the answer. He had switched to their security service division—and yes, by golly, now I mentioned it, the record showed he was one of the night-duty guards at the Crowder mansion."

Altman forgave Dr. Fields. "What I really wanted to do was kiss him," Altman said. "When those gardeners' prints turned out clean, I felt my heart go way down. I had been just so damn certain it was one of them. But there you go. Cops and their one-track minds."

A bearded night guard by the name of Howard Plumpton turned out to have Alan Crowder's fingerprints. He denied he was Alan Crowder and he denied any involvement in the threats and other things that had happened to Harry. He was taken downtown and questioned for two hours by four detectives who kept talking over one another and never addressed the prisoner in anything less than a shout. Finally he cracked.

"He told us he was Alan Crowder," Altman said. "His buddy Howard Plumpton had died in a fire back in 1974. Some very heavy people were homing in on Alan at that time, so the opportunity for an exchange of identities was a godsend. Not that it didn't trouble him to do a thing like that, he added, as if that might make us believe he was a good guy at heart."

As Plumpton, Alan Crowder had steered clear of the law and had even managed to hold down some good jobs over the years, though never for long. He never forgot his brother, and the way Harry had turned his back on him, and he dreamed of having the chance to get back at him one day.

"I started hanging round Bel Air when I read Harry was moving there," Alan said in his statement to the LAPD detectives. "I signed up with the agency that supplied gardeners and such, knowing they would most likely be approached for staff at the Crowder place. Sure enough two gardeners were hired. I wasn't one of them, but a little bribe to the right guy got one of them replaced, and for a few weeks I was right there, pulling Harry's weeds and watering the flowers."

He knew his brother would be spooked by the notes, he said, because Harry had always been susceptible to the mysterious and the unexplained—"One of his many faggoty touches. I guess with the nasal spray thing, I went too far, I knew it as soon as I did it, but I couldn't get in and snatch it back. A gardener has good cover until he leaves the garden, right? So he took it, it hurt him bad, and I thought, Christ, I'm supposed to be playing with his mind, his real weak area, so I made myself cool it, and I came up with the liquorice poisoning instead. That took some doing, but by then I was a security guard—I bribed the same individual at head office and got transferred to security the same week Harry got the number of guards increased."

Being caught by his fingerprints, Alan admitted, was not something he had considered. He had believed that the way things had been planned and executed, no one would come under suspicion, and brother Harry would turn his back on everybody, like he always did, and the torture could go on, sporadically, for as long as he wanted to keep it going.

"After the fourth note, I was going to leave it for maybe a year, anyway," Alan said. "I realised I was doing something that gave me real satisfaction. The way I figured it, if I could go on, over the years, timing the renewed assaults just right, I could go on torturing Harry for the rest of his life. I'm sorry it didn't work out that way. He's a bastard, and I would still like to rob him of every shred of happiness. That's my dearest wish."

Alan was tried on charges of causing bodily harm, committing malicious mischief and impersonation. He was sentenced to 18 months in the state penitentiary.

"Outside the court," Altman said, "Harry waited for the prisoner to be brought out. When Alan came down the steps between a couple of guards, Harry asked if he could have a word. They said they'd give him one minute. So Harry asked Alan two things: first, had he been the mysterious woman opposite the gate?

"Alan grinned and said yes, he was. The veil was a nice mysterious touch, he said, but it had been more practical than anything, because it covered his beard.

"The second thing Harry wanted to know was, could he assume it was over between them now? Was the slate clean, was the score even? I was watching Harry, I could see this really mattered to him. Alan could see that, too. He smiled at his brother and he said, 'They told you what my dearest wish was, didn't they?' Harry said sure, the cops had told him. 'Well then,' Alan said, 'I guess that's still my dearest wish. I'll be seeing you, Harry.'

"They took him to the van and Harry Crowder stood there and stared as they banged the doors shut on his brother. He looked terrible. In fact he looked so bad I offered to drive him home, but Audrey Neal was waiting for him and she drove him away."

Alan Crowder served ten months of his sentence in the state penitentiary. His dearest wish was never realised, however: his brother died of a ruptured cerebral aneurysm six months after Alan was imprisoned.

TEN

MOTHER FIGURE

From time to time there are cases where the police are in no doubt that a crime has been committed, and that a particular person is guilty, but they find themselves powerless to make an arrest. The case of Mary Stonemuir almost fitted that category.

In 1981, the population of the village of Barnwell, near Cambridge, was increased by one when Eddie Hoskins, a retired civil engineer, took on a housekeeper to help look after him and his picturesque home. Copton House stood at the rear of its own half-acre of land, on the edge of a wood at the western side of the village. It was a painstakingly converted seventeenth-century barn; there were four bedrooms, two bathrooms and a central great hall, with dining and drawing room areas partitioned off with fine antique panelling; the large kitchen retained the period style of the rest of the house, but in functional terms it was entirely modern.

People in the village were surprised that Eddie, a lifelong bachelor with the reputation of being a woman-hater, had taken on a housekeeper, and such an attractive one. Mary Stonemuir, a Scot from Edinburgh, was 42, rather tall with a fine figure and striking auburn hair. She had delicate, regular features and spoke with a soft voice that was slightly accented. People tended to remark on her amber eyes, which gazed steadily when she spoke. The local vicar, Arnold Kemble, found that talking to Mary was a mesmeric experience.

"With as much honest hindsight as I allow myself," he said, "I have to say I was partly smitten with her. She was a beautiful woman and it went right the way through—her deportment and her voice and her intelligent style of conversation were all perfectly matched to her appearance. A person like that, if she had been the woman she seemed to be, would have been managing a business somewhere, or running a successful college for young women."

Detective Superintendent Ralph Gillett, who would later investigate the disturbing events at Copton House, said that "professional misfitting" was one of the commonest giveaways among people with criminal natures.

"You come across it all the time. There'll be a fraud, say, and right there in the firm where it happened there will be somebody doing a job that he seems much too good to be doing, and as often as not he'll turn out to be the villain. A colleague on the Scotland Yard Obscene Publications Squad says it's often the case with perverts, too. You'll get this really smooth managing director type, elegantly dressed, perfectly groomed and with excellent manners, and you learn to your surprise that he's a hotel doorman, and he gets his jollies fumbling little boys."

In spite of appearing over-endowed for the job she was doing, Mary Stonemuir was well liked and trusted by the villagers at Barnwell. During her first month at Copton House she was invited to a number of small social events, and although she never accepted any of the invitations, that didn't stop people asking her.

"She was like one of our own," the postmistress said. "Fitted in from the first day she was here. I'm sure there wasn't a soul that disliked her."

Two months after Mary Stonemuir arrived in Barnwell her employer, Eddie Hoskins, fell ill. He was visited at home by Dr. Michaels, a general practitioner who served Barnwell and two neighbouring villages.

"Eddie had been on my list of patients for twenty-three years," Michaels said, "but that was the first time I'd seen the inside of his house. It was a magnificent place, light and airy, and the housekeeper had filled it with flowers and strategically positioned plants. A really happy place, it seemed, and the housekeeper herself was an absolute charmer."

During the visit Eddie told Dr. Michaels that Mary Stonemuir had previously kept house for the Earl of Aykebridge in Somerset. She had left when the Earl's daughter came back from American and insisted on running the house herself. Eddie said he had been really lucky to get somebody like her to look after him—he had been prepared to accept the services of any nondescript old woman who could prove she was honest and fit enough to do the job.

"My wife had been dead for a year at that point," Michaels said, "and I can remember how I envied Eddie, because I was planning to hire a housekeeper myself, but I hadn't got around to advertising for one. Who knows, I thought, if I'd advertised sooner, I might have got Mary Stonemuir. God, just think. I was actually jealous of the poor man . . ."

Eddie appeared to be suffering from some kind of debility. He had never suffered any illness other than childhood measles, colds and two bouts of influenza, but now, at the age of 66, he appeared to have fallen prey to an infection that made him feel too weak to stay out of bed for long. He also complained of headaches, occasional dizziness, nausea and drowsiness. Mary Stonemuir said he hadn't been eating especially well for some days, and he had been complaining of feeling faint.

"My assumption, initially," Dr. Michaels said, "was that he had contracted a low-grade viral infection. I told him to stay in bed and I'd call back in a few days."

Three days later Eddie began having hallucinations. His brother, Jack, who was visiting from his home in London, called Dr. Michaels.

"By this time Eddie was feverish and rambling,"

Michaels said. "He kept rubbing his stomach, groaning and talking in breathless sentences that meant nothing. I took a blood test and sent it off for priority analysis."

The haematology laboratory noted the presence of a foreign element in Eddie's blood, but they couldn't say what it was. A consultant haematologist put forward the possibility that it was a toxin being manufactured by a virus colonising Eddie's liver or spleen. He recommended a biopsy.

"Biopsy involves removing a tiny portion of tissue for examination," Michaels said. "In Eddie's case that meant cutting out pieces of his liver and spleen. It was a job that had to be done in hospital, so I booked him in. His brother Jack was very worried by this time. The housekeeper kept a discreet distance all the time, only speaking when she was asked something. I remember thinking, fleetingly, that Jack gave the impression he didn't like the housekeeper—and that was odd, because everybody for miles around, including me, thought she was the bee's knees."

When Eddie was in hospital being prepared for a liver biopsy, he suffered a seizure that resembled an epileptic fit. His teeth clamped together so tightly and so abruptly that he bit through the tip of his tongue, severing it. The rhythm of his breathing began to fluctuate and then it suddenly stopped. Strenuous efforts were made to revive him, but after twenty minutes he was declared dead.

The following night Jack Hoskins put in a brief appearance at the pub in Barnwell. He had two large whiskies, and halfway through the second he looked across the bar at the landlord and said, "I know that bloody woman did for Eddie, and I'm going to prove it."

He said no more. He left the pub a few minutes later and drove back to his brother's house. When he got in, he later reported, the housekeeper was in bed. He went to Eddie's study and opened the desk with the keys his brother had always carried in his pocket. He went through the various insurances and among them he found a detailed set of instructions, in Eddie's handwriting, on what should be done in the event of his death. Beneath that he found a photocopy of Eddie's will.

"Jack Hoskins was a friend of Commander Douglas, one of my superiors," said Detective Superintendent Gillett, "and the commander asked me to go and see him, he was very distressed. I went to his brother's house at Barnwell and the housekeeper showed me in. I found Jack Hoskins sitting in a big winged armchair in the study. I told him who I was and without further ado he showed me the will. It was straightforward. Jack was to receive a lump sum of money. The house, the land and the bulk of Eddie's other property all went to Mary Stonemuir."

"He knew the bitch barely two months," Jack told Gillett.

The Superintendent tried to be diplomatic. He pointed out that it wasn't unknown for a man to leave everything he possessed to a woman he had fallen for, however short the acquaintance.

"Speak to her," Jack said. "Just speak to her. She won't say a word to me. If you speak to her you'll know there's something up. That cow murdered my brother."

Gillett said he understood that Jack would be feeling upset at the loss of his brother, but he couldn't go around throwing out wild accusations without something concrete to back them up.

"My brother was fit as a horse all his life," Jack said. "This woman shows up and suddenly he's ill, and just as suddenly he's dead. Then it turns out she's inherited most of his money, a magnificent house and a highly desirable piece of land. Things just don't happen that way. He was manipulated, then he was killed."

After cautioning Jack once again to guard his tongue, Gillett went to the kitchen and spoke to Mary Stonemuir.

"She was an incredibly calm and self-possessed woman," Gillett said. "She almost made me feel I was the one being scrutinised. I told her she wasn't under any suspicion, but that in view of inferences that might be drawn in this and that quarter, perhaps she should talk to me about her relationship with Eddie Hoskins. Well, she looked at me with those steady amber eyes of hers and said, 'We were lovers.'

"She didn't even blink. I said I found that hard to believe—they had only known each other a few weeks, after all, and Eddie Hoskins was known to be a man who made friends slowly, and who furthermore had never befriended more than a couple of women in his life. 'We met a couple of years ago,' she said. 'In France. We were both on holiday.' She said they became lovers at that time, and since then Eddie had visited her regularly at her home in Cheltenham, but soon after he retired he persuaded her to move in with him. Neither one of them wanted to get married, she said, so they decided she would pass herself off as his housekeeper, for the sake of appearances."

Mary Stonemuir also told Superintendent Gillett that she had not wanted Eddie to leave her anything in his will, but he had insisted, because he said she had done more to make him happy than any other person in the world.

Gillett couldn't help remarking that for a lover so recently bereaved, Mary was remarkably composed.

"I was brought up never to show my feelings to strangers," she told him coolly. "Eddie's death has been a terrible blow to me. That doesn't mean I have to add a loss of dignity to a broken heart."

Gillett did not immediately tell Jack Hoskins what Mary had said. He foresaw a nasty scene if he didn't get Jack out of the house first. They got in Gillett's car and he drove them to the pub. There, in a quiet corner, he repeated Mary's story.

"Jack went ballistic. He banged the table, he swore, he spilled his drink and had to go and get another. He was now more convinced than ever the housekeeper had done-in his brother. When he calmed down a bit he asked me what I thought. I told him it was too early to say what I felt. We had to wait for the result of the autopsy on Eddie before we even began to form hard opinions. I told Jack all that, but really I believed there was something very far wrong about Mary Stonemuir."

The autopsy was inconclusive. It said Eddie's intestinal tract showed signs of severe irritation, but neither the blood nor the stomach contents provided any clue as to what had made him ill and finally killed him.

"Around six o'clock on the day the autopsy results were issued," Gillett said, "I got a call from a forensic toxicologist, Desmond Stuart, who told me he'd been contacted by the pathologist who carried out the autopsy on Eddie Hoskins. Stuart said the pathologist thought there was something deeply suspicious about the condition of the body. Nothing he could pinpoint, but it wasn't right. Stuart was going to have a very specialised look at the blood and stomach contents and some samples of tissue. He wondered if he could talk to me about the case first. I said I'd be happy to accommodate him, but first I had to make sure Jack Hoskins was behaving himself."

Jack was now living in bed-and-breakfast accommodation at the pub in Barnwell. He told Gillett that Mary Stonemuir had asked him to leave the house. Gillett was not surprised. He asked Jack to promise he wouldn't cause any trouble in the meantime, and to help make him feel better, he explained that a specialist in poisoning was now getting involved in the case.

"That cheered Jack up, he felt his suspicions were

being taken seriously. I went into Cambridge and met up with Desmond Stuart. When I had given him the whole story, which admittedly wasn't much, he thanked me and said he would be in touch, just as soon as he had examined the specimens taken from Eddie's body."

Stuart issued his report four days later. In part it read:

My analysis of blood samples from the deceased shows the presence of the poisonous elements to be found in the vegetable species Datura, Hyoscyamus (Henbane), the common potato, and Woody Nightshade. Datura is poisonous in all its parts and contains the alkaloids levohyoscamine, atropine, and hyoscine or scopolamine. The lethal dose of these three alkaloids is about 1 grain for adults and 0.1 grain for children. The action is slow and a fatal issue may not occur for days or weeks. The other vegetables, the potato included, contain solanine, which is a poisonous narcotic alkaloid obtained from potato sprouts and tomatoes. The symptoms of poisoning are dryness of the mouth and throat, visual hallucinations, mental excitement, temporary lapse of memory, nausea, vomiting, abdominal pains and distension, and fading of vision. The deceased showed all these symptoms, and postmortem findings in the body tissues support the probability that the poisons in his system were the primary cause of death.

Desmond Stuart later told Superintendent Gillett that
he also found traces of hyoscine in the blood samples,
but that they hadn't been evident at the time he made
his report.

"Hyoscine is rarely used homicidally, he told me,
but in the case of Dr. Crippen's wife, it was thought
to have been the cause of death."

Gillett was anxious to know how Mary Stonemuir,
assuming she was the poisoner, would have obtained
the substances used to kill Eddie Hoskins. Stuart replied that the police should look for a herbalist or
some such skilled practitioner somewhere in the
woman's background.

"These poisons, especially in combination," Stuart
said, "are very hard to locate at autopsy. I had to
employ some fairly tricky tests to determine they were
there, and then a few more tests to find out what the
substances really were. If this poisoner had been just
a little bit better at the job, we probably wouldn't have
found a clear cause of death."

Gillett asked what Stuart meant by "a little bit
better."

"The person who uses poisons of this type can rely
on them eventually disappearing from the body as
long as the victim is alive," Stuart said. "The trick is
to administer the cocktail of poisons in such a way
that it does fatal damage, but not so swift in its action
that death will occur before every last trace of the
poisons has left the victim's body."

Gillett got a search warrant and a team of four detectives searched Copton House. Mary Stonemuir

stood in the hall throughout the search, staring out of the window. After three hours of searching, the team left. They had found nothing.

At approximately this time it occurred to Superintendent Gillett that Jack Hoskins had been keeping a low profile. Gillett asked for him at the pub and was told he hadn't been around for two days. The landlord reported that after a fairly long lunchtime drinking session, Jack had announced suddenly that his brother had never been to France in his life, which mystified the landlord; he also announced he was going up to the house to have it out with that murdering cow. He had left at once, and he had not come back yet. His bags were still upstairs at the pub, and he had paid for the room to the end of the week, two days after the provisionally scheduled time for Eddie's funeral.

Superintendent Gillett organised a search for Jack. "I didn't think I was being unreasonable. I have enough instinct to know when something's gone wrong. After two days of searching, Jack was officially posted missing."

Gillett went to Copton House and questioned Mary Stonemuir. She was uncooperative; the few answers she provided were entirely negative. Gillett told her that he believed she had murdered Eddie Hoskins, and he was beginning to think she had a hand in the disappearance of Jack Hoskins, too. Mary told him she had never heard such nonsense in her life.

"We were now running extensive checks into the background of Mary Stonemuir," Gillett said. "Apart from the circumstantial facts which made it clear to me that she had murdered Eddie Hoskins, we had nothing at all that could be used towards a prosecution. Eddie had died of poisoning, but there was no proof that she had administered it, or that there had ever been any in the house."

There was no record of a Mary Stonemuir in Edinburgh, and when the referees' names on her CV were checked, it was found they didn't exist; the Earl of Aykebridge in Somerset was a fiction like all the others.

"I got a forensic psychologist to go with me when I confronted Mary with this," Gillett said, "and with the fact she was unknown in the city she claimed was her home. All she did was shrug. I think she knew exactly where she had us, which was up a blind alley. We could show she had falsified her CV, and had told a few lies about where she came from, but so what? There was nothing there she could even be arrested for. In the opinion of the forensic psychologist we could grill Mary all we liked and for as long as we liked, she was not the kind who would ever crack. 'She's devoid of scruple,' he said. 'I've only ever seen the type twice before. She gives me the creeps, if you'll pardon the unprofessional tone of the evaluation. In my view she is capable of anything, anything at all if it serves her ends.' "

Over the following days small plastic bags of minced human flesh and bone began turning up in rivers in Buckinghamshire and Hertfordshire. Each bag contained only a few ounces of the decomposing material, and by the time it occurred to Superintendent

Gillett that this might be the mortal remains of Jack Hoskins, the police had collected more than thirty bags.

"We couldn't be sure it was Jack Hoskins because there were no identifying characteristics," Gillett said. "Mince, after all, is mince, but we were sure it was him all the same, and we were sure Mary Stonemuir had despatched him. While she was off attending Eddie's funeral, we searched the house again, quite illegally this time, and we searched the grounds, too. It took sixty men more than an hour, and we found nothing."

It is inevitable when the police are frustrated in their enquiries, and when their only suspect appears to have stymied their enquiries completely, that they will begin to assume the suspect is invincible.

"I certainly believed that," Gillett said. "Against my will, of course—and I hardly admitted it to myself—but the fact was, we had one murdered victim, probably two, and a woman we were *certain* had done it, and we had knocked ourselves out trying to get just one clue, anything at all, and we had failed, and every time the suspect saw me or any of my men she just smiled her aloof smile and passed by. Oh, it was galling. I felt utterly defeated. We all did."

And then a pair of hands turned up. They were found in a trap, inside a drain twenty feet to the rear of Copton House, by a service engineer who had come to fit a new garbage disposal unit.

"We should have twigged that, but we didn't," Gillett said. "There had been a garbage disposal unit at

Copton House, the kitchen sink was specially adapted. The only thing was, last time we searched, there was definitely no garbage disposal unit. For whatever reason, Mary Stonemuir had got rid of it.

"We could speculate about the amount of mince you could produce by adapting a garbage disposal unit, of course, but for the moment that was by the way. We had a pair of human hands! And they were from the drain at Copton House! Evidence of a felony at last, and it was firmly linked to Mary's dwelling place."

The hands were badly decomposed, and when a pathologist examined them, he found they had no skin.

"This was a double blow," Gillett said. "We knew Jack Hoskins's fingerprints were on record, because he had been a CND campaigner in the sixties and had been arrested for assaulting a politician, but there were no prints on these hands. Once again Mary had slipped out from under. There was a small consolation this time, however; she had *only just* managed it."

Desmond Stuart entered the picture again. He had a side interest in the identification of decomposed and waterlogged remains, and had been instrumental in identifying several bodies dragged from rivers around the county. He examined the bloated hands, procured samples of the tissue and took them back to his lab. Two hours later he was on the telephone to Superintendent Gillett.

"I believe these hands have been boiled," he said. This added another bizarre layer of speculation to the police theories of just what Mary Stonemuir had done to Jack Hoskins's remains. Gillett asked Stuart if that information had any special significance.

"It could mean," Stuart said, "that if the hands were relatively intact when they were thrown away, the skin would subsequently slip off, just like gloves, after they began to decay. You should get your chaps to dig around in the sludge at the bottom of that drain trap and see if they can find something like a very slimy old pair of grey gloves."

Before Stuart rang off, he told Gillett he believed the reason they had been lucky enough to obtain the hands was that, as sometimes happens with bulky garbage, they had popped out of the waste-disposal grinder and gone into the drain relatively undamaged.

A late-night torchlight search of the drain was made, with Mary Stonemuir watching from a window. Something roughly like a bundled pair of slippery, foul-smelling gloves was found. They were taken straight to Desmond Stuart's laboratory. He was called at his home and came at once.

"What he did astonished me," Gillett said. "He put on a pair of tight rubber gloves, then he slipped the skin from the hands over his own hands, like a second pair of gloves. He then rolled ink carefully on the fingertips and made a set of prints."

They matched the record of Jack Hoskins's prints. Mary Stonemuir was arrested. While she was being read her rights she calmly sipped a cup of tea. She got into the police car without protest. By the time they arrived at the police station four miles away, she was dead.

"The cup was examined later," Gillett said. "She had spiked the tea with aconite. Enough to despatch a pony."

Strenuous efforts to identify Mary Stonemuir were fruitless. No record of her existed anywhere; no one recognised her photograph, her fingerprints were not on file, and no record could be found of her dental pattern.

"There was a hell of a lot we wanted to know," Superintendent Gillett said, "but we never found out any of it. To this day, Mary's picture is hanging in my successor's office, her dead face calmly staring out, like it's defying anybody to hang a history on it."

ELEVEN

PREJUDICE

Cerebral palsy," said Dr. Ferenc Mora, "has been the dominant barrier of my life, and it has certainly limited my growth as a working professional."

Dr. Mora was talking in 1990, the year he retired as principal of the Debrecvanya Institute of Forensic Services in central southern Hungary. During the second half of his career, Dr. Mora distinguished himself through inspired investigative work in a number of difficult police cases, and by publishing a forensic technicians' guide to animal hair analysis, which ran into several foreign language editions and won Dr. Mora two scientific writers' awards in Hungary. He died less than a year after he retired.

"His achievements were outstanding by any standards," said a colleague, "but when you take into account that he was always a severely handicapped man, with practically no control over his body, his accomplishments have to rank as phenomenal."

Dr. Mora was always completely objective about his condition. "I cannot walk, I have to be wheeled everywhere. My head shakes about wildly at times, my speech can be understood by only a few very patient individuals, and I have to use other people's handling skills to perform much of my work. Yet the condition has not been such an obstacle as some would think. I am a fulfilled forensic investigator, and my work has served the course of justice in Hungary for twenty-six years."

Dr. Mora's close personal assistant, Dr. Margarita Szabo, vividly described both the condition and the extent to which it affected her boss.

"Cerebral palsy is a loss of voluntary control over the movements of the body, resulting from a brain disorder suffered either before birth, during the birth process, or during infancy. The term cerebral palsy usually includes all motor difficulties that can be attributed to a cerebral disorder in early life. Generally, though, two types of cerebral palsy are meant by the term. One is spastic, the other is athetosic. In the spastic type, the voluntary movements are severely paralysed, with spastic contraction of the arms and legs. In the athetosic type, the voluntary movements are often not paralysed, and the spastic signs may be very slight, or they may be absent. Instead, there are slow, mobile spasms in the face, neck, arms and legs, either on one side or, more often, on both sides. There is involuntary movement in the whole body, with grimacing and garbled speech. Dr. Mora's condition contains a measure of both spastic and athetosic characteristics. It takes people a while to get used to him, but the time spent is always rewarding. He is a fine and remarkable human being."

Dr. Mora always believed that handicaps could profitably be regarded as disguised opportunities. "None of the ordinary activities like sport or dancing or the pursuit of young women were ever likely to make calls on my time. My condition helped me to be single-minded and focused in my approach to a problem. All in all I was able to follow my professional leanings with little in the way of distraction."

There was one severe drawback, however, that he regretted every day of his life, and he knew how it pained other sufferers. "The greatest burden of the condition, from a sufferer's point of view," he said, "is the difficulty of communication with other people."

A case in which Dr. Mora's work was preeminently successful was also one where, because of mindless prejudice, a child's cerebral palsy lay at the heart of an act of calculated savagery against an innocent person.

On a freezing morning in February 1989, a farmer called Zsigmond Heltai telephoned the police and told them he had received a death threat. Inspector Sandor Miricz went out to the farm with two of his men to investigate. The farmer, Heltai, took them to a field

half a mile from the farmhouse and pointed to a stake
sticking in the ground.

"It wasn't there last night," Heltai said.

The police officers took a closer look. Stuck on top
of the stake was a piglet's head, and stuffed in its
mouth was a note written in thick black letters which
said, SOON THIS WILL HAPPEN TO ANOTHER
PIG.

In Hungary, as in several other countries, the word
"pig" is offensive slang for a policeman. Heltai was
a part-time volunteer police officer whose enthusiasm
for the job was known to have made him enemies in
the local community.

"I told Heltai we would pass along the note to the
forensic people," Inspector Miricz said, "and in the
meantime he was to try not to worry. I pointed out
that less than one in a thousand death threats are ever
carried out, but Heltai said it wasn't just himself he
worried for. He had a wife and a disabled daughter to
think about."

The note was passed to the Debrecvanya Institute
of Forensic Services, where it came under the scrutiny
of Dr. Mora.

"There was no chance at all of gaining an identification from the writing," he said. "The letters were
large and they had been gone over again and again,
so that any natural tendencies of letter shape and pencil pressure were disguised by the repetition. The paper was from a cheap notepad and the pencil could
have come from anywhere. We opened a folder on

the case and filed the note. For the moment that was all we could do."

Next day Heltai called Inspector Miricz and told him he had been threatened over the phone. The caller had been a man, he said, and he had told Heltai that it wouldn't be long, they were closing in on him.

"Again, all I could do was try to reassure the man," Miricz said. "It still only sounded like a threat campaign, something cooked up by a disgruntled petty criminal to annoy Heltai."

That evening Greta, Heltai's wife, arrived home with their daughter Magda and found that a brick had been thrown through the farmhouse window. At the sight of the damage the child became distressed and hysterical.

"Magda was a sensitive girl," Inspector Miricz said. "She was 12 and perfectly intelligent, but she had been born with cerebral palsy. She was severely spastic on one side and had to be wheeled about in a chair. Emotionally she was very fragile. She was overwhelmed at the sight of the mess, the ripped curtain and all the broken glass on the living room floor. It was too much for her."

The child was still being placated when Miricz arrived at the farmhouse. He told Heltai to sit down and make out a list of all the people he could think of who might wish him harm.

"It could be a long list."

"Make it as long as it needs to be," Miricz said. "I think it's time we talked to some villains."

The list, when it was complete, contained the names

of well-known minor criminals and troublemakers; it also had the names of two local businessmen. Miricz took Heltai aside and asked him about that.

"You asked for the names of people who wish me harm. One of those men, Myrmus, is my former bank manager. He got very upset because I went over his head when he turned me down for a loan. I got the loan and he got a rap on the knuckles for failing to encourage borrowing by people with collateral."

"And the other one?" Miricz said. "Zoltan Brody's a lawyer, isn't he?"

"That's right. He's also the husband of a woman with whom I had an affair. It ended two months ago; she told him about it and I know he's been seething ever since."

Miricz took away the list. "I planned to send out officers to interview everybody who was named," he said, "not so much to learn anything as to pass on the warning that the police were now involved, and we wouldn't be long in catching up with anyone who thought he could take the law into his own hands."

That same night, less than an hour after the child Magda had finally been quietened and was asleep in her bed, Greta Heltai heard a gunshot. She rushed out of the house and saw her husband walking towards the gate. In the light from the kitchen door he looked pale and frightened.

Inspector Miricz returned to the farmhouse and noted the details. Heltai had been walking along the path from the livestock sheds when he heard a sound in the bushes. He turned, was momentarily aware of a reddish glint, then looked down and saw a red spot glowing on the front of his coat. He had heard of the Russian laser-sight rifles being sold in the region and knew immediately what was happening. He dropped to the ground just as a shot was fired.

"I heard it whistle over my head," he told Miricz. "Some crazy bastard tried to kill me."

The following morning, Greta Heltai could not start her little car. That was annoying for a number of reasons. For one, the car was specially adapted, with a space in the front where Magda's wheelchair could be positioned, and for another they were already late, as Magda had been sick that morning and had needed to be bathed twice.

"I almost didn't take her to school, but she insisted she wanted to go," Greta said. "So when the car wouldn't start, I got my husband's keys, put the wheelchair in the boot of his car, carried Magda across and strapped her into an adapted baby-chair he had rigged for her in the back seat. It wasn't such a good arrangement as putting the wheelchair into the car, but the important thing was, it was safe. When Magda was securely belted in I got in myself."

When Greta turned the ignition key, the car blew up. She remembered nothing of the event, but Magda did, and she was able to tell one of her teachers, who transcribed her statement for the police.

"I was strapped in the back of the car, and I was slipping down because the seat was too big for me; it didn't hold me up the way my wheelchair does. I was going to call Mummy and tell her I was sliding down and couldn't see out the window, when there was a big bang, the car jumped up and came down again and there was lots of smoke. I screamed, I couldn't stop myself. It was all dark in the car, there was smoke everywhere and it hurt my eyes, and I started to cough. I think I heard Mummy then, she was crying, shouting my name, telling me it was all right."

A bomb had gone off under the driver's seat. It was made from a steel pipe packed with explosives and dozens of fragments of metal. The detonator was wired to the car's ignition. The blast drove a total of sixteen pieces of steel and rusted iron into Greta Heltai's lower body.

"I don't know how she did it," Inspector Miricz said, "but she undid her belt, pushed open the car door and crawled out. I think it must have been hearing Magda in the back, trapped and screaming—it must have fired something primal in Greta and she got the other door open before she passed out. People on a neighbouring farm heard the blast and came running."

They found Greta lying face down by the car with blood oozing from her terrible injuries. Magda was screaming in the back and smoke billowed from the remains of the front seat.

"It looked as if the car had been hit by a mortar," one of the rescuers said. "We got Greta and the little girl away from the wreckage, in case the fuel tank caught fire. Zsigmond Heltai came running across the fields just as the ambulance arrived. He was screaming louder than the little girl—he could see the mess his wife was in and he thought she was dead. To tell the truth, we didn't think it would be long before she was."

Over the next month Greta Heltai underwent twelve operations for the removal of metal fragments from her body, and six further procedures to correct the massive damage done to her abdomen and legs. Every night her husband sat by her bed, holding her hand, telling people over and over that the bomb had been meant for him.

"We rounded up everybody on Heltai's list, of course," Inspector Miricz said. "As we expected, the bank manager and the lawyer were incensed and threatened to bring actions for defamation. The others, villains for the most part, denied any knowledge of the events at Heltai's farm. While we were checking their alibis and trying to give the impression we were on top of the case, Dr. Mora and Dr. Margarita Szabo were looking at the evidence."

The bomb fragments from the car and from Greta Heltai's body were assembled in the laboratory and scrapings were taken from each.

"Dr. Mora felt it was important that a scientific identity be established for each fragment," Dr. Szabo said. "He ordered a spectrographic analysis of every item, and as each analysis slip came in it was stuck on the left-hand page of an open ledger. After a couple of days Dr. Mora suggested we go out to the farm. We took with us a mechanic, who examined Mrs. Heltai's car, the one that wouldn't start. He found straight away that it had been tampered with—there were pieces of paper over the ends of the plugs, so no power could get through.

"Meanwhile I pushed Dr. Mora round the outbuildings in his wheelchair, and as we went he would point to scraps of metal about the place, and I would pick them up and put them in a sample bag slung on the back of his chair. He also asked me to pick up several samples of earth, quite at random."

The metal fragments were taken back to the laboratory and scrapings were taken. These were sent off for spectrographic analysis at the same metallurgical research station as before. The earth samples were analysed in Dr. Mora's own laboratory.

"Simultaneously, we were analysing the explosive used in the bomb," said Dr. Mora. "In the blackened casing we found traces of nitro-glycerine, cellulose nitrate, sodium nitrate and charred wood pulp. That combination told us it was gelignite. A second analysis, geared to estimating the proportions, gave us a figure which we could check against a list of manufacturers' specifications. That way, we soon knew who made the stuff, and that information set the police on the road to finding out who bought it. They would also be helped in this by the fact that a brass serial tag, of the kind often wired to bundled sticks of dynamite, was picked up at the scene of the explosion."

It was six weeks before Greta Heltai left hospital. Her daughter Magda had in the meantime been taken into the care of a local children's hospital, since Zsigmond Heltai had not felt able to look after her on his own. The reunion between mother and daughter was deeply emotional. Later the same day, Inspector Miricz asked to see Greta in his office. He sent a car for her and a wheelchair was used to bring her from the car to the office. Miricz apologised for putting her to such stress on her first day out of hospital.

"But it's important you know what we have been able to determine about the terrible thing that happened to you."

That same morning, Miricz said, Dr. Mora and his team had issued an interim forensic report on the car bomb.

"The first thing you should know," Miricz told Greta Heltai, "is that the bomb was made at your farm."

Greta said she didn't understand.

"The casing, and the fragments that filled it, all came from the farm. The metal fragments carried traces of minerals from the earth around your yard— but more importantly than that, the metal pieces, all of them, came from the accumulation of metal scrap lying around in the outbuildings. There can be no doubt of that, Greta."

She told him she still didn't understand. What exactly was he telling her?

"Then there's the matter of the explosive charge," Miricz said. "Gelignite, sold to the lawyer Zoltan Brody." At this Miricz noted that Greta looked startled. "What is it?" he asked her.

"He said he had forgiven my husband."

Now Miricz watched Greta turn defensive. She had

not intended to say anything about her husband's affair with the lawyer's wife. "It's nothing," she said quickly. "Another matter entirely."

"The gelignite was bought for the purpose of removing a giant tree stump from Mr. Brody's garden," Miricz said. "He did not plan to use it himself, as he did not know how. He bought the gelignite and delivered it directly to his gardener. We have made thorough enquiries and we have determined that this is entirely true. It is also true that one stick of the gelignite was stolen from the gardener's locker, situated in a shed at the bottom of Mr. Brody's garden."

Miricz said no more. He sat back and waited for a reaction. Greta was silent for several seconds.

"You are telling me that my husband stole the explosive from the garden shed at the home of his mistress, and he used it to make the bomb that nearly killed me." She looked at Miricz. "That is what you're telling me, isn't it?"

"The deduction is hard to avoid, Greta."

"There's no possibility of a mistake?"

"Dr. Mora is one of the best forensic men we have. He has double-checked everything." Miricz paused, making sure Greta was in control of herself. "Can you think of a reason why your husband would want to kill you?"

Greta nodded. She said she could think of three reasons. "And in time they probably became one big reason, fat and tight and imperative."

Again Miricz waited. Greta seemed to droop where she sat.

"Since the time we were married, my husband has always believed that I rejected him sexually. He said I did not respond to his lovemaking the way a woman would who truly enjoyed it. I tried to tell him that noisy overt response was not my way, but he was obsessed about it, and when our child was born, and it was discovered she had cerebral palsy, he said I had subconsciously done that to humiliate him still further. It sounds crazy, it probably is unbalanced to some extent, but he did, *does* believe that Magda's condition is my rebuke to his unsatisfactory prowess as a lover. When I tried to make him understand how ridiculous that was, he said women could do these things without knowing how.

"Then the full resentment of the situation gushed out of him all at once. He reminded me that he had said he wanted a son. That was true, he said he wanted a son and I told him if it was to be, then it would be. But in my rejection of him and his feeble sexuality, as he put it, I not only didn't give him a son, but the daughter I gave him was damaged."

Greta sat in silence for a while. Miricz got her a cup of coffee and sat at his desk again. "You said three reasons, Greta."

"His lover. She wants him to run away with her. I know my husband's psychology, or enough of it to be aware how he thinks in a crisis of loyalties. With me dead there's no wife to betray. That may sound bizarre, but we're both aware, I think, that Zsigmond's mind travels on bizarre lines. He would sooner cancel me than abandon me."

"The affair with the lawyer's wife—it isn't over?"

"He wants everybody to think it is. He even convinced her husband it is, but no, it's not over."

"And reason number three?"

"The money. I have a life insurance that would make him rich."

It was decided that Greta should return to the hospital for the time being, until the police had made their next move, which would be to bring in Zsigmond Heltai for questioning. Inspector Miricz arranged for a hospital suite where Greta and Magda could both be cared for, then he called together the squad working on the Heltai case and discussed the interrogative approach they would use on the farmer.

The meeting was just winding up when a call came in from a lookout posted near the farmhouse to watch Heltai's movements. The lookout reported that three minutes ago a car had drawn up outside the farmhouse and the lawyer, Zoltan Brody, got out. He went to the door and knocked loudly. Zsigmond Heltai opened the door, they exchanged words, then they went inside.

The lookout was still delivering his report when there was a sound of gunfire from the farmhouse. A moment later the door burst open and Heltai staggered out. Blood streamed from cuts on his face, his arms and his chest. He was carrying a shotgun.

A police patrol was on the scene within two minutes. Heltai was taken to hospital, suffering from multiple deep cuts and a stab wound to the shoulder. In the farmhouse the police found the dead body of Zoltan Brody lying in the hallway. He had a sharp craft knife clutched in his hand. He had been shot in the chest with a shotgun.

Miricz arrived at the scene shortly after Heltai was taken to hospital. He looked at the blood on the kitchen floor and the overturned furniture. "Leave everything just as it is," he said. "I want Dr. Mora to take a look."

At the hospital, Zsigmond Heltai received more than 200 stitches to his wounds. He was told he was lucky to be alive, he had lost nearly three pints of blood.

When Inspector Miricz arrived to question Heltai, he had decided that for the moment, he wouldn't mention the bomb and what they now knew about it. He would not mention, either, that the dead lawyer's wife was at that moment being questioned elsewhere.

He asked Heltai to tell him exactly what had happened.

"It was horrible," Heltai said, lying back in the hospital bed, bandaged to the neck. "There was a knock at the door. I answered it and Zoltan Brody was standing there. He said he had to talk to me, it was important. I invited him in and offered him a glass of wine. He said no, there would be no time for that. Then he pulled out a knife and he attacked me with it. I kept running away and he ran after me, flailing at me with it, cutting and slashing me. He kept screaming he was going to kill me. I stumbled into the broom cupboard in the hall, trying to keep away from that damned knife, and I found myself holding my shotgun. I picked it up and levelled it at him. I warned him to back off or I would shoot him. He sneered at me and said I wouldn't have the nerve. That was when he reached out and stuck the knife in my shoulder. The gun just went off, it was a reflex. He was standing right in front of it. I watched him fall, then I started to feel very sick. I realised for the first time how badly I was injured. I went along the hall and opened the door. That's all I remember, until I woke up in here."

Dr. Mora spent two days examining the house, in the company of his assistant Dr. Szabo. They took another day comparing Heltai's account of what happened with the evidence of their forensic sweep of the farmhouse, and with the surgeon's report from the hospital. Two more days passed before Dr. Szabo came to Inspector Miricz's office to tell him what they had found.

"It's all in the report," she said, putting a fat folder on the desk, "but to save you the tedious detail, I can tell you the important stuff. First of all, the wounds on Zsigmond Heltai. We studied the surgeon's detailed evaluation and discovered that the wounds all had one thing in common—they were deeper at their lower points than at the middle or upper point. This is consistent with self-inflicted wounding. So is the distribution of the wounds, and the way they tend to be deeper on the left side of the body than on the right—because Heltai's right-handed, and his stronger, more adept right hand did all the damage on the left side of his body.

"Next, he says he was chased. Well, the blood spots

in the kitchen are typically those from a stationary subject. A moving man who happens to be bleeding will leave elongated splashes of blood on the walls and floor; they would look like exclamation marks turned on their sides. The blood deposits at the farmhouse are all either round, or star-shaped, which are the two main shapes made on the floor by blood that has fallen straight down from a static or nearly static subject. Dr. Mora believes Mr. Heltai walked slowly round the kitchen, cutting himself, letting the blood drip down. What he should have been doing was running round the kitchen like the wind, sticking the knife into himself every way he could."

"What was the lawyer doing all the time this deliberate cutting was going on?" Miricz asked.

"I was coming to that. He was actually lying on the floor, unconscious. Heltai, we believe, must have been waiting for Mr. Brody to show up, and he had a club ready. Actually it was a rolling pin; we found it in the drawer, and there was a smear of blood on it which has turned out to be the same as the lawyer's. So Heltai waited for the victim to show up, he invited him in, hit him on the head with the rolling pin, then took his time to cut himself up. When he was done, he picked up the gun and shot the lawyer dead.

"That was another thing. He said the lawyer was standing in front of him when he shot him, but a substantial number of pellets penetrated the man's chest, and we would have expected to find them in the wall, or in the woodwork, or the furniture. But no, they all smacked into the linoleum on the hall floor. The angle of the shot shows that if Mr. Brody had been standing when the shot was fired, Heltai would have had to be down on the floor shooting upwards."

Miricz was impressed. He thanked Dr. Szabo and asked her to convey his congratulations and his gratitude to Dr. Mora.

"There are two things more," Dr. Szabo said. "The knife in the dead man's hand was lying loosely between his fingers. That wouldn't have been the case if he had been holding it when he was shot. He would have had it in a tight grip, the so-called death grip."

"What's the other thing?"

"Remember the note that was left in the piglet's mouth? We took away the notepad from the hall table and did an infra-red impression test on it. There's a clear imprint of the death threat, and I think we've even got the pencil he used to write it."

Later in the day, a detective reported that the widow of Mr. Brody told him that on the night her husband called on Heltai, he had received a call from the farmer asking him to come round to discuss something important. The woman admitted she was planning to run away with Heltai, but she swore she had nothing to do with what happened to Greta Heltai. The detective didn't believe her, but he would work on that aspect of her statement later.

At the hospital, Zsigmond Heltai was confronted with what Dr. Mora and Dr. Szabo had found. Heltai denied everything. He said it had happened exactly as he had told the police. He was then told that his lover had been talking to detectives all day. Heltai fell quiet, then asked to speak to a lawyer.

As Inspector Miricz was leaving he succumbed to an unprofessional impulse. He asked Heltai how he could have done such a thing to a fine woman like Greta—and how in God's name could he have done it knowing that his helpless daughter would also be in the car.

Heltai looked at him. "That thing is not my daughter," he said. "Daughters are human."

"And what is Magda, if she's not human?"

"A useless troll."

Miricz found that the unprofessional impulse persisted. He stepped back into the room and stood at the foot of Heltai's bed.

"You'll go to prison for the rest of your life for what you did," he said. "And do you know something? The man who got the goods on you, the man whose talent will put you where you'll never do harm again, is another troll. Just like little Magda."

TWELVE

BAD BLOOD

St. Luke's Place in New York has always been a highly desirable spot to live, and Sidney Loomis knew that. The place where Sidney lived wasn't at all desirable, it was a cold-water apartment off Cranberry Street in Brooklyn, only half a mile from the slum tenement where he was born. Sidney was 26 and, even though he had been sure since boyhood that he would end up living somewhere elegant and grand, he still hadn't managed to get out of Brooklyn.

Several times a month he would put on a clean shirt, a sports coat and a tie, get on the subway and ride across the city, just so that he could walk along St. Luke's Place, soaking up the atmosphere. He had told his wife that sometimes he would pretend to himself he lived there and was out taking a stroll before dinner.

He knew all about the street. On the north side there is a row of fifteen elegant houses, all dating from the 1850s, and Sidney had a list of the famous or powerful people who had lived there over the past hundred years. Opposite the houses is a park named after Mayor Jimmy Walker, who once lived at Number 6. Sidney could tell his friends that the house on the block that is best known to the public is Number 10, because on television it is shown as the home of the Huxtable family in *The Cosby Show*—even though the series is allegedly set in Brooklyn. Sidney could also point to Number 4 and tell anyone who was interested that the movie *Wait Until Dark*, starring Audrey Hepburn, was filmed there. A writer called Theodore Dreiser—Sidney had to admit he had never heard of him—once lived at Number 16, where, around 1925, he wrote his novel *An American Tragedy*.

Sometimes Sidney would stand outside Number 16, staring at the attractive door, imagining he was a famous writer, or a banker, or anything famous or powerful enough to make him respected. He imagined that he lived in there.

"The kid was an incurable dreamer," said Marvin Travis, deputy manager at the electronic assembly plant where Sidney worked. "The real world hardly touched him. The other world, the place in his head, was always getting between him and what he could see and touch and smell. He wasn't stupid, though. People made that mistake. They thought he was dumb."

Marvin recalled Sidney's first day on the job.

"He had to learn to solder, and it's an easy enough job to do, but because we do contract assembly work, the job calls for more than one kind of soldering, so new employees have to bone up a little on the strict procedure side, just so they'll know that whatever the contract, whatever the size or number of the components, the job will consist of the same seven steps, every time.

"I sat Sidney Loomis down and gave him the spiel. I told him soldering is a process that uses metal alloys with a low melting point to join metal surfaces without melting them. He seemed to take that in.

"So then I gave him the basic operational steps; I told him exactly what his job would be, all day and every day. Step one, clean the surfaces to be joined, using chemicals or abrasives, whichever the job called for; two, put on a flux to remove the oxides on heating, and to help the solder to spread; three, line up the parts to be soldered; four, apply the heat; five, feed the solder to the joint; six, cool the joint without moving it—and last of all, seven, remove any residue of flux from the joint.

"Well, that was the whole meatloaf, the total of what he needed to know and needed to do to keep himself in a safe little job for as long as he wanted it. Now I didn't expect him to reel it all right back at me. I would have expected him to stick on a point here and there, first time around, but when I asked him to repeat what I had just told him, he couldn't think of anything. It was like somebody wiped his memory clean."

Marvin Travis was to learn that Sidney could sometimes appear to be attentive and alert, when in fact he was daydreaming. "And he would go off into a dream at any time, there was no rule, no special set of circumstances."

In ordinary circumstances Sidney would not have been taken on at the factory, but at the time of his interview they were experiencing a small boom, and they needed extra hands, urgently, to cope with a sharp rise in the volume of contract work coming in. Sidney was told again what his job entailed, and a woman took him through the process several times, showing him how to handle the equipment and perform the few simple manoeuvres.

"The thing was," Marvin said, "once he got the hang of it, that was that. He would sit at his bench and plough through his day's work without a squeak or murmur. He never got bored, never complained, never goofed off. For six whole months he was the ideal guy for the job. God knows where he got to in his head, and frankly I didn't care. He earned his money and never caused us a minute's trouble. I suppose I should have realised it wouldn't last."

In 1994, a year before he started work at the electronics assembly plant, Sidney was married to Dorothy, a waitress he had dated a few times and decided he loved. Dorothy was a hard-working young woman with no firm belief in her own worth. She had married Sidney, she told a friend, because he was good to her and had never tried anything funny on any of their dates. She also said that Sidney reminded her a little of Brad Pitt, although her friend could not see the resemblance.

Six months after Sidney started the soldering job, Dorothy gave birth to a baby girl. They called her Denise, after Dorothy's mother, and for a time Sidney lost his preoccupied air. He would talk to people at work and tell them all about the baby, about the way he could get her to sleep in four minutes flat, how she would recognise him and smile as he approached her cot even though she was so young. He told them about feeding her and bathing her and putting a fresh diaper on her all by himself, two evenings a week when Dorothy went round to see her mother.

"He was a very happy father," Marvin Travis said. "Sickeningly so, in the opinion of some people, but I thought it was an endearing thing, that innocence of his. He told people that now there was a kid to be responsible for, he was setting his sights high. He planned to take a home-study course in accountancy and get himself registered. Then he would go to work for one of the Wall Street firms and he would work all the hours he could and he would save, save, save. Then, by the time his daughter was old enough to go to school, he would send her to one of the good ones, somewhere handy to the new place they would be living by then—St. Luke's Place, of course. There would be no half measures, nothing but the best would do for the Loomis family, and I'm sure he believed he'd make it."

One night on the way home from work, Sidney thought he saw Dorothy standing across the street, talking to a young man in a light raincoat. It was raining and as Sidney watched he had to wipe the rain from his eyes several times because it kept obscuring his vision. Poor visibility or not, he was convinced it was Dorothy he saw across the street. As he stood by a lamp post and watched, the young man put his arms around her and kissed her.

Sidney was so shocked that he looked away. When he looked again they were gone. He hurried home and Dorothy was there as usual, stirring the evening meal on the two-ring cooker.

"He asked me where I'd been," Dorothy later told the police. "I told him nowhere, I hadn't been out. It was pouring with rain, I wouldn't have gone out in that, especially not with the baby."

That evening Sidney was quiet. After dinner he sat holding the baby for a while, staring at the television, either too deep in a daydream to hear the occasional tentative question from Dorothy, or deliberately ignoring her.

"He was definitely upset," Dorothy said. "I'd never seen him that way before, he was always even-tempered, never up or down. That night he went to bed early and later, when I got in beside him, he was still awake. In the dark he asked me who it was I was talking to on the street. I told him again, I hadn't been out, it must have been somebody else he saw. He said no, it was me all right, I was out in the rain and I didn't have Denise with me, I must have left her in the apartment. I said he was crazy to think I would do anything like that. He just turned over and didn't say anything more. Next morning he got up and went to work without speaking to me or kissing me good-bye. He had never done that before."

Dr. Jason Kelly, a forensic psychiatrist who would later examine Sydney, said he appeared to have developed a delusional system that drew heavily on his store of daydreams.

"It would have been relatively easy," Dr. Kelly said, "to draw up a list of clinical features and perform a mental status examination on Sidney. In my view that would have demonstrated that he was suffering from a delusional state, a powerful one. However, there was so much about Sidney that was unique that I didn't want to submit him to standard testing and content myself with a stock determination of what was wrong. I took my time and treated his case as something rather special."

Sidney's habit of projecting himself into fictional situations had undermined his capacity to tell truth from unreality, Dr. Kelly said. "Not always, of course, but at times where his deeper emotions were engaged. Seeing a young woman across a rainy street who resembled his wife in some small way—that was enough to start up the delusional mechanism. His mind was well tuned to taking the bare bones of reality and converting them into something else, something unreal that nevertheless had the vividness of reality. I have no doubt that the young woman and young man he saw on the street really did embrace and kiss—Sidney took that much of the reality and projected his beloved wife into it, making it a powerfully affecting scene—and totally convincing."

Sidney began to behave differently at work, and Marvin Travis had his own way of describing what was going on.

"He'd spent so much of his time away from reality, he couldn't find his way back any longer," Marvin said. "The first wrong thing he did was to take a circuit board and put a bridge of solder across two components that shouldn't have touched each other at all. That one mistake seemed to set the pattern; he didn't just do it on one board, he did it on a whole day's batch. I know now we should have been checking his stuff at regular intervals, but we were really busy, and Sidney's work was usually so good, we relied on him to turn in a perfect job, time after time.

"These were expensive boards I'm talking about. Since it was his first mistake on the job, it was decided he wouldn't be fired. I took him on one side and laid into him, giving him all the heavy warnings I could think of, and realising all the time he wasn't really hearing me."

The next day, halfway through the afternoon, Sidney stopped the job he was doing and approached one of the other workers, Ricky, a young man he sometimes sat with on the lunch break. He asked if he could see the magazine Ricky had shown him the week before. Ricky had a collection of magazines in his locker, most of them pornographic. He asked which one Sidney meant.

"The one with the chart in it."

"Chart? What chart?"

It was in the back of one of the magazines, Sidney said. It was a chart explaining to the reader how to tell if a baby was his. Ricky asked him why he wanted to see that and Sidney said he just did, he was interested.

"I had to tell him to wait until break time," Ricky said. "He was impatient, he'd obviously got something on his mind and he wanted me to go and find the magazine straight away and bring it to him. The boss was watching us by that time so Sidney backed off, but I could see he was all on edge, dying to get his hands on the chart."

In the lunch break Ricky went to his locker and started going through the magazines. Sidney stood behind him, shifting from foot to foot. Finally, Ricky found the magazine he wanted. Sidney said he didn't want to take the magazine home with him, because of its lurid content, and asked if he could cut out the chart instead. Ricky said that was fine by him.

The chart was headed, IS THAT CHILD REALLY YOURS?, and it consisted of three columns: the first showed the possible matings between different blood groups—for example, Group O with Group O, Group O with Group A, Group O with Group B, and so on; the second column listed corresponding blood-group possibilities among offspring, while the third column listed the blood groups which could not be formed from particular pairings.

Before Sidney left work that evening he went to the personnel office and asked if he could see his employment record card. He was told that the original card was stored elsewhere, but a copy of it could be called up on the computer. The clerk asked him what he wanted to know.

"My blood group," he told her.

The clerk entered Sidney's name and ran the personnel database. "Your blood is Group O," she told him.

When Sidney got home he ate his dinner in silence and afterwards rummaged through baby Denise's records from the hospital where she was born. Later still, he asked Dorothy if she happened to know her own blood group.

"I asked him why he wanted to know," she said. "He told me he just did. So I told him I was Group O. He nodded and went quiet again."

Sidney sat down and wrote out the simple facts he had gathered about the blood grouping of his little family. He was Group O, Dorothy was Group O, and Denise was Group A. According to the chart, the child could not be his. A Group O father and a Group O mother can only produce a baby with Group O blood. To produce a baby with Group A blood, Dorothy would have had to mate with a man also having Group A.

Sidney went to bed early. When Dorothy got up next morning he had already left, but he did not go to work. Instead, he went to St. Luke's Place. For a long time he stood outside Number 16, where the famous writer had lived, and he stood staring at the front door. Eventually a police officer came along and asked him what he was doing.

"Just looking," Sidney said.

The officer told him to look elsewhere. Sidney went away. He took the subway back across town and walked to the corner where he believed he had seen Dorothy with the young man in the light raincoat.

Sidney stood on the corner and waited. According to eyewitnesses he was there for more than two hours, not moving from the spot, occasionally stamping his feet and shrugging his shoulders against the cold, but never taking his eyes off the front of the building across the street.

Much later, Sidney would tell the forensic psychiatrist, Dr. Kelly, that he saw Dorothy again, with the same young man, who appeared to work in one of the offices in the building across the street. This time Dorothy was more cautious; she stood back in the shadows of the doorway and when the young man kissed her again she drew him in beside her, so they wouldn't be visible.

"But I saw them," Sidney said. "I don't know how she thinks she could make me believe it was somebody else. I know my own wife when I see her."

That night he asked Dorothy why she had gone out and left Denise on her own again. Dorothy said she hadn't done that. He argued that he had seen her, and when Dorothy got tired of denying she had left the baby, she went to bed. Sidney woke her up and told her he knew everything.

"I know Denise isn't my baby," he said.

Dorothy told him that was a horrible thing to say. He said yes, it was, and he hated saying it, but it was true, he knew it was true and somebody was going to be sorry it was true.

"You won't be able to stand in the street necking with him any more."

Dorothy began to feel scared. Sidney meant her no harm, she was sure of that, but he obviously intended to do harm to somebody. She told him he wasn't well, he should see a doctor. For the first time since she had known him, she saw Sidney turn angry. He picked up a cup and smashed it against the wall. Then he grabbed his coat and stormed out of the apartment.

That night he did not come home. Dorothy called Marvin Travis next day and asked if he had seen Sidney. He said no, he had been planning to come round to see what was wrong—this was the second day Sidney hadn't shown up for work.

"Maybe I should talk to the police," Dorothy said.

Marvin said that sounded like a good idea.

"I'd already quizzed Ricky and found out about Sidney being anxious to lay his hands on the paternity chart," Marvin said later. "You hear a thing like that, and you realise something really bad is going down. Sidney had never been the most regular of boys, but for a while he was all on the bright side, there was no darkness about him. Lately, it was different, he looked preoccupied the way you always imagine molesters and muggers look. Something was eating his brain—and next thing I hear is, he's checking up on the paternity of his kid. I didn't say anything to his wife about that. I just prayed it was a feature of his low mood that would go away before any harm got done."

Eight hours later, the body of a young man wearing a light-coloured raincoat was found in the doorway of the building where he worked, a few blocks from the cold-water apartment where Sidney, Dorothy and Denise lived. The dead man was Roy Carson, a claims adjuster with an insurance company.

A hot-dog vendor told police that he had seen the dead man being approached by another man. "It was the same guy that stood on the corner near my stand two or three days ago," he said. "He was there for a couple of hours, watching for somebody."

Other eyewitnesses provided the police with descriptions which all roughly coincided. Within an hour Sidney was in police custody.

"Interviewing him was a pretty unusual experience," a homicide detective said. "He denied any knowledge of what happened to Roy Carson. He was convincing enough, too, except you could tell he was drifting off some place else in his head. He was like a junkie, without the stoned aura."

Later Sidney was interviewed at length by the forensic psychiatrist, Dr. Kelly. He freely admitted to Kelly that he had been watching Carson misbehaving with Dorothy.

"He talked and talked," Kelly said, "although he

skirted any admission of involvement in Roy Carson's death. He stopped in the middle of it all and said to me, 'This is like the confessional, right? It's sacred, you can't say anything to anybody else.' I was happy to let him think that, but he still didn't make a confession."

The police had very little evidence to work with. Roy Carson had been saying something to Sidney Loomis. There had been no apparent contact between them, and it was only some time after Sidney had walked away that someone realised Carson was lying in the doorway where he had been standing a couple of minutes earlier.

"Sidney said he recalled asking someone the time," the detective said, "but he had no idea who it was, he didn't remember even looking at the guy's face."

Two pathologists from the Medical Examiner's Department performed an autopsy on the body of Roy Carson. They could not find a cause of death.

The senior pathologist reported that there were no marks of violence on the body. "The heart appeared congested, and there was some suggestion of paralysis in the lungs, but those are signs that usually *accompany* some other manifestation. We're not accustomed to finding them on their own, so to speak. All we could say, really, was that the man had died suddenly."

Blood and tissue samples were submitted to extensive testing. Two chemists were sure they detected traces of unusual chemical compounds, but they couldn't agree on their findings. In the meantime, a young forensic chemist, Paul Darbon, went to the place where the body was found and looked around for anything that might suggest a line of enquiry.

"I was there," Darbon said, "because one of the pathologists told me, off the record, that the body looked all wrong for a natural-causes death. What it did look like, to him, was a poisoning. Poisonings happen to be my enthusiasm, and I love a challenge."

In an alley beside the office building Darbon dug around in a trash can and found an empty whisky bottle. He sniffed it and automatically recoiled.

"I moved so fast and with such instinctive panic, I didn't even get the smell past my nose before I was blowing it out again. It was one smell I know to steer away from. Mind you, the concentration by that time was very low, it probably wouldn't have hurt me."

Darbon took the bottle back to the laboratory and performed a couple of swab tests on the few drops of liquid in the bottom.

"It had probably been full before, but it had been emptied into the trash and the contents had been dissipated and corrupted by all the decayed and semi-decayed matter. There was no use me trying to get any more evidence from such a tainted source. What I needed to do, I knew, was make some connection between Sidney Loomis and the substance I had found.

"I sat down and looked at the evidence that had accumulated on the case—which wasn't much—and I read the police interview notes on Sidney Loomis.

When I saw where he worked, something occurred to me."

Darbon went to the plant where Sidney worked and asked the deputy manager, Marvin Travis, if there was such a thing on the premises as a case-hardening unit for metals.

"We do have such equipment, yes," Marvin replied. "It's kept in an isolated area, of course. Can't be too careful."

"And the cyanide?" Darbon said.

"That's kept in a locked cabinet in the basement."

Later Darbon told the police, "Cyanides are used in a number of chemical processes, including fumigation, case hardening of iron and steel and electroplating. Specialist and contract electronic firms often keep small-scale plant for the preparation of metals. I'd say I was playing a hunch rather than a long shot. When we went down to the basement to check on the cyanide, the cabinet had been forced. About an ounce of cyanide was missing."

What Darbon had smelled in the bottle from the trash can was the almond tang of cyanide and a strong whiff of vinegar. When any acid—vinegar included—is mixed with cyanide, the combination produces hydrocyanic acid gas. One sniff of the freshly generated gas can be instantly fatal.

"And Sidney Loomis had been warned about that," Darbon said. "As part of his initiation process, he had been cautioned against touching any of the chemical compounds on the premises. Marvin Travis had decided to drive the message home by explaining how simple it was to make a lethal mixture without trying too hard. The illustration he used was a real case from his previous place of work, where a technician threw a beaker of acid solution into a sink that contained a residue of cyanide solution. The combination produced hydrocyanic acid gas and the technician fell down dead the instant he inhaled it."

Now that the pathology technicians knew what they were looking for, they applied the appropriate test procedures. The lung tissue from Roy Carson's body tested positive for hydrocyanic acid.

"I believed that Sidney Loomis had walked up to his victim with the lethal mixture in the capped bottle," Darbon said. "He then held his breath, uncapped the bottle, and held it under Carson's nose. That's all it would have taken. Sidney would have to do no more after that. Then he could simply walk away and ditch the bottle."

The police called at Sidney Loomis's apartment. He wasn't home. Dorothy hadn't seen him since he had been taken away for questioning. A description was circulated, and three hours later a patrolman called in a report of a dead body in the park at St. Luke's Place. The homicide detective who had questioned Sidney arrived and was shown the body, curled up under a blanket beneath a tree. It was Sidney. There was a note pinned to his lapel. It said:

I wanted it all to be past and forgotten, but I could not forget. The thinking of it hurts me and it will not stop.

An autopsy showed that Sidney had swallowed cyanide.

"He would never have believed that the young man he killed was innocently waiting in that doorway for his girlfriend, who worked in a building further along the street," said the forensic psychiatrist, Dr. Kelly. "He would never have believed, either, that he was wrong about Denise not being his child. Dorothy was a good and loyal wife. The clerk in the personnel department at his place of work was not as efficient as she might have been. When she told Sidney he was Group O, she was reading from someone else's record. The autopsy proved beyond a doubt that Sidney's blood was Group A."

THIRTEEN

A LOSS OF FAITH

In 1978 the Spanish resort of Orilla Blanca, on the Costa del Sol, was just beginning to attract holidaymakers in numbers that would support a civic expansion programme. Plans were being drawn up for improved public amenities, school extensions were proposed and there was a detailed plan for a local welfare scheme for the elderly and disadvantaged. At the same time licences were being granted for the building of several hotels along the *Loro Verde* and *El Gozo* beaches.

"Naturally, money going out meant money had to come in," said Tomasso Ligueres, at that time a member of the Orilla Blanca Civic Planning Authority. "We tried to be sensible and make sure that the rate of intake was higher—by about 30 per cent—than the rate of outgoing. That way we improved our community and got a healthy bank balance at the same time."

One man who benefited unofficially from the improving fortunes of Orilla Blanca was Eduardo Pereda, an official at the Secretariat of Land Franchises. Pereda negotiated rents and leases with hoteliers, restaurant owners and shopkeepers.

"It was a job which he had been allowed to create for himself," Ligueres said. "The expansion of business in the town was faster than a lot of people expected. It caught the civic administrators on the hop; we suddenly needed new and more streamlined means to cope with the influx of trade. Pereda had been in local government for a number of years, and he had negotiated many of the rents and leases for existing hotels and shops. When it came to appointing someone to oil-up the mechanism of licensing and fee collection, Pereda was a natural choice. It was a long time before anyone caught on to the scam he had set up for himself."

In the summer of 1978 Eduardo Pereda's wife, Isabella, gave birth to their only child, a daughter called Ingrid.

"You could see straight away that she would grow into a fine-looking woman," said Ligueres. "By the time she was seven or eight she already had the classic Castilian look, the finely-sculpted features, the alabaster skin and jet-black hair. I think her mother decided she saw something too vulnerable in all that beauty, and that is why she put Ingrid's education in the hands of the Church."

From the age of 7 until she was 17, Ingrid spent eleven months of each year with the sisters at the Convent of the Blessed Saint Catherine, high up in the hills of Sierra Llana to the north of Orilla Blanca. The sisters were kind to her but their educational regime was strict. When Ingrid finally left their care she was considered to be a well-educated and religiously devout young woman.

"She looked like a saint, too," Ligueres said, "but in a decidedly arousing way, if you know what I mean. The girl exuded a kind of purity that was sexually charged. She had an extraordinarily fine figure, her face was a dream—and on top of all that she dressed modestly and carried herself demurely, like a good Catholic girl should. The combination was irresistible."

Ingrid would promenade round the square in traditional fashion with her father and mother each evening, and on Saturday nights they would dine together at a fine old restaurant in the centre of the town. People were so impressed with Ingrid, Ligueres said, that they stared at her openly.

"Modest reticence and physical beauty are a rare mixture. Within days of returning to the family home she had several admirers, bold young men with rich fathers, but Ingrid's mother kept them at bay. Isabella had plans for her daughter that did not involve letting her marry any man from the Costa, however well-off his family might be. The immediate plan, as I understood it at the time, was to send Ingrid to work for an old-established firm of lawyers in Barcelona, who had already interviewed her and were prepared to employ her as soon as she turned eighteen."

Two weeks before Ingrid's eighteenth birthday, a team of auditors from Madrid descended on the Secretariat of Land Franchises at Orilla Blanca. They had come at the invitation of two senior local-government accountants who had detected irregularities in the way land rental and property leases were administered. The auditors examined the complex contractual arrangements and the equally intricate system of banking carried out by the Secretariat. They found more than irregularities. In the words of the senior auditor, the system of rents and lease payments was designed to bleed two to three per cent of the cash intake along convoluted channels that all led to one place—Eduardo Pereda's pocket.

"It was a terrible scandal," Ligueres said. "They found that Pereda had inserted contract clauses and banking instructions into the complicated web of the departmental procedures. The word 'obfuscation' was used several times in the auditors' report. That was very apt. Eduardo Pereda had used the dense fabric of his department's working methods to obscure his own villainy."

The sudden loss of his respectable status was more crushing to Pereda than the prospect of a long prison sentence. He became deeply depressed. Late one night, a police officer looked into the cell where Pereda was being held, and saw that he looked unusually still. A closer look revealed he was dead. He had taken a belladonna plaster from a carbuncle on his shoulder and soaked it in his drinking water. He then drank the powerful solution of deadly nightshade and probably died within minutes.

The effect on Pereda's wife was devastating. In the space of ten days she had lost her husband, her financial security and her social standing; in a few more weeks she would lose her home. Ligueres believed that bereavement, shame and worry combined to unhinge her mind. She gave Ingrid a case with all the money she had set aside over the years—406,000 pesetas, about £2,000—and told her to go to Barcelona at once. Ingrid did not want to go, but her mother insisted.

Ingrid left for the big city, and two days later her mother sought sanctuary with the nuns at the Convent of the Blessed Saint Catherine. The retreat did not bring her the spiritual peace she needed. She had been at the convent less than a month when she threw herself from a window into a deep rocky ravine. The fall did not kill her. She suffered serious head injuries and spent the remaining years of her life in a vegetative condition, never speaking and never appearing to recognise anyone who visited her.

In Barcelona, Ingrid rented a small flat and began working for the firm of lawyers. In the evenings she prayed and read religious books. She struggled to understand God's purpose in destroying her family, and when she could not do that, she tried to make herself accept that she had no right to question what had happened; she must simply accept.

But she could not do that either.

"I answered an ad she placed in a news kiosk for someone to share the flat," said Emilia Bazan, a hairdresser who had recently come to the city to work in a department store. "I was desperate for somewhere decent to stay, but at first I thought I wouldn't want to live with Ingrid. The shelves were full of holy books, and she had statuettes of Christ and the Blessed Virgin all over the place. She dressed a bit old-fashioned, too. I decided I'd give it a month's trial, and if it didn't look like it was working out, I would have enough time to find somewhere else before I moved out."

The two women got on well, however. Ingrid needed companionship, and for the first time in her life it came from someone her own age. In a short time she had opened her heart to Emilia, telling her how she felt her childhood and early teen years had been wasted, how she had been shut away with musty old nuns and fed brain-stunning nonsense about sin and guilt and everlasting damnation.

"They taught me that God is omnipotent," Ingrid told Emilia, "which means that he is all powerful, that he can do or undo anything. Nothing is beyond the reach of his influence. They also told me God is good. Well, what I say is, he can't be both good *and* omnipotent. If he is omnipotent he could have stopped my father from going wrong and dying the way he did. He could have stopped my mother turning herself into a vegetable. But he didn't stop any of it, did he?"

Emilia had to agree, the Almighty hadn't stopped the misery.

"So if he could stop it, but chose not to, then he isn't good, is he?" Ingrid said. "Not my idea of good, anyway, and my idea of good is the same idea of good that's handed down by God's gloomy servants. On the other hand, if he wanted to stop it but couldn't, that means he isn't omnipotent."

Emilia had been so impressed with the argument that she made Ingrid repeat what she had said and wrote it down. Ingrid, for her part, was fascinated by Emilia's worldliness.

"She wanted to know how long I'd been going out with men, what I did when I was with them, all the details of a date. It was incredible—it was 1996, she was 18, and she hadn't been out with a boy, never mind a man."

Emilia said she would take Ingrid with her to a dance. First, though, they would go to the store where Emilia worked, and where she got discount, and they would get Ingrid something decent to wear.

"In a miniskirt and a little cut-off top she looked fabulous," Emilia said, "but I had a hard time convincing her. She decided to go for something less extreme, a knee-length skirt and some v-neck tops, really cool-looking stuff. She wore some of it to work at the lawyers' office, just to get used to the feel of it, and the female manager told her to go home and get changed into something decent."

Emilia believed that incident finally turned Ingrid

around. She came storming back to the flat at lunch time, while Emilia was there making herself a snack.

"She sat down at the table with her bank statements and payslips and did a couple of quick sums, then she told me that was that, she was giving up the job. She had enough money left to live on for seven months. That would give her time to find a better job."

The changes in Ingrid after that were rapid and numerous. At the second dance she attended with Emilia she accepted a lift home from a good-looking young man with a vintage MG sports car. Next day, a Sunday, she told Emilia he had invited her to lunch with his family.

The family turned out to be the young man, who was called Gabriel Borea, his father Pascual, and his mother, Dorita, who had had a stroke and needed to be fed by a maid.

They had lunch on a balcony overlooking twenty-six acres of grapevines. Gabriel explained that his father, who was an older image of Gabriel, produced wine that was used in hotels and restaurants all over Spain and the Canary Islands.

"Ingrid told me she noticed that after lunch Gabriel wheeled his mother away and rather pointedly left her alone with his father," said Emilia. "She was sure it was done deliberately, she had seen Pascual make eye signals to his son."

When they were alone Pascual talked for a while, moving his chair over beside Ingrid's. He told her about his bottling plant and the old wood barrels he still used and had to restore all the time, and the other barrels, the new ones that were made of stainless steel and hardly needed any maintenance. As he talked he let his hand rest on Ingrid's arm. A short time after that his hand was on her knee, and she felt she had no power to resist.

"Then he sat back quite abruptly," she told Emilia, "and he took a little card from his shirt pocket and gave it to me. He said if I would meet him at that place on Wednesday at one, he would treat me to a very special lunch, much better than the one we'd had today."

Ingrid admitted she was smitten by Pascual. He was perhaps 50, she wasn't sure, but he was handsome and probably the most charming man she had ever met.

"Are you going to meet him on Wednesday, then?" Emilia asked.

"Oh yes. I wouldn't miss it."

"What about Gabriel?"

Ingrid shrugged. "He doesn't seem to mind. He didn't even drive me back here, one of the servants brought me."

On Wednesday Ingrid had lunch with Pascual. The next evening they had dinner. On Friday night he took her to a club, and she didn't return to the flat until morning. When Emilia asked her coyly where she had been all night, she said Pascual had taken her to his apartment in town.

"That was all she would tell me," Emilia said. "She had coffee, had a shower, then went to bed for the rest of the day."

Ingrid continued to see Pascual for another four or five weeks. Emilia saw less and less of her. She slept during the day and went out every night. When Emilia suggested they have a night on the town together, Ingrid said that would be nice, but she took it no further.

Then one day Emilia saw an open-top Bentley go past the store where she worked, and she was sure she saw Ingrid sitting beside the driver. He was a man of about 60, bald and rather fat. He drove with one hand and had the other arm around her shoulders.

"I didn't say anything to her about that," Emilia said, "but a while later, maybe a week, I saw her in a coffee shop near where I worked, and she was with *another* old guy. This one was really gross: he had a blue mouth, like he was going to drop dead from a heart attack any minute, and his neck was like rolls of fat piled on top of one another. He was sitting opposite her at a table near the window, and she had on this big fixed smile, and he was pawing her hand on the table. It was really disgusting, her being so pretty and delicate, and that old pig looking at her like he couldn't wait to do something unspeakable."

At approximately that time Ingrid visited a priest. He had seen her on two previous occasions in his church, sitting in a pew, staring at the altar.

"She was such a striking young woman, it would have been hard not to notice her," the priest said, "but apart from that, the look on her face was quite arresting in itself. She did not look troubled, as some people do when they come to sit in the church. I'd say, rather, that she looked bewildered. The way visitors to the city look when they get lost. I saw her twice, and I decided that if she came a third time, I would speak to her. It has never been my policy to force my help or comfort on anyone, but there is such a thing as responding to an evident need for contact."

Ingrid did not wish to make her confession, she simply wanted to tell the priest something.

"I have heard some terrible things in my thirty years in the priesthood," he said, "and at other times my heart has been wrenched by the depths of misery I have been compelled to witness. This young woman, however, moved me in another way."

The priest invited her into the sacristy, where they could talk without being overheard. He noticed as she sat down that she looked incredibly weary for such a young person.

"I was startled by what she said. She told me she had become detached from her faith. Those were her words and that was how she appeared. She was like an amputee, missing a part of herself, displaying a kind of vapid, understated grief."

She had obviously thought the matter over, the priest said, and she spoke with great clarity. She told him that she had, in the first place, rejected her faith. Her family had been disrupted, destroyed, and she could see no purpose in that, nor any hint of God's compassion. Things she had done since rejecting her faith had completed the detachment. The priest didn't press her to say more on the point, she simply told him she had done some very wicked things. She was beginning to miss the comfort of her faith, but she had discovered it was not something she could simply take up again. It had gone. Her capacity for belief and for dependence on the Christian ideal had evaporated.

"It felt terrible, she said. It felt as if she had been cast adrift. She was an educated young woman, I could easily tell that, and I could tell she was well schooled in the observation of Catholic ritual. A loss of faith in that person—a person whose mind and spirit had been attuned to a life of religious observance—must have been a dreadful state of affairs."

The priest asked Ingrid what he could do to help her. Nothing, she said. She had wanted to tell him, that was all, because she felt it was important to express her loss of faith to someone who listened and perhaps understood.

The priest told her he would pray for her.

"She moved out of the flat on a Tuesday," Emilia said. "She told me the place was now in my name, and the rent was paid up for three more months, so I could take my time to find someone new to share the cost of the place. I thought I was going to cry. For a time we had been great pals, and I'd thought we could be again. She had grown distant, though. She still smiled, she was still the same bright girl in lots of ways, but there was a change and it made all the difference. She packed her things, a chauffeur came and took them away, and that was that. She had moved out."

Three days later Ingrid's body was fished from the harbour.

"Superficially, there wasn't a mark on her," said

Dr. Pedro Lammas, a senior forensic pathologist with the Catalan Institute of Criminal Investigation. "The body had not been long in the water—it had been spotted by a fisherman returning in the early light and he had pulled her on board his boat. She was naked. A subsequent trawl of the harbour failed to locate any clothing."

Under the powerful lighting of the autopsy room, Dr. Lammas and his assistant examined every inch of Ingrid's body. They took scrapings from under the fingernails, where tiny deposits of debris were visible.

"So often these scrapings prove to be nothing but dirt from the water which clings to the oiliness at the junction of the nail and the fingertip," Lammas said, "but we would never assume it was unimportant."

After swabs had been taken from the body orifices the autopsy commenced. Lammas had first of all to determine if Ingrid had died of drowning. This is not always easy to prove, one way or another.

"The idea to grasp," Lammas said, "is that when a living human being actually dies in water which contains diatoms—they're microscopic algae—many of these diatoms will penetrate the tissues of the lungs and get carried to other organs such as the brain, the kidneys, the liver, and even into the marrow of the bones.

"After the autopsy, samples of these organs can be soaked in strong acid to dissolve away the soft tissue, thus leaving the highly-resistant diatom skeletons to be identified under the microscope.

"Now, when a dead body is put in the water, or

when death in the water is not caused by drowning, then, although diatoms may get to the lungs, the fact that there is no heart beat means the diatoms can't circulate to other organs."

The diatom test is still controversial. Some scientists argue that diatoms can get into the body by other means than drowning. However, practical pathologists like Lammas favour the use of the test as a reliable indication of drowning, though not as legal proof.

"The tests showed there were diatoms in the lungs, but none were located in the brain, liver, kidneys or bone marrow. My conclusion was that Ingrid Pereda had not died of drowning. She was almost certainly dead before she entered the water of the harbour."

The tissue of the lungs and the heart muscle showed signs of congestion, consistent with undue pressure. The probable cause of death was suffocation, and that probability was strengthened when the blood analysis results indicated a high concentration of cocaine in the bloodstream. Cocaine intoxication, Lammas explained, renders a user susceptible to suffocation very much more easily than an individual without the drug in his or her bloodstream.

Analysis of the body-orifice swabs revealed traces of semen in Ingrid's vagina, anus and mouth. The scrapings from under the nails were largely insignificant debris. There were however a number of tiny fibres, identifiable as short acrylic strands, fawn in colour.

"I have known times," Dr. Lammas said, "not so many years ago, when we would have been arguing as to whether the young woman had drowned or not. We would have been mystified by the presence of substances in the blood we could not identify, and the material from under her nails would have had no significance, because we simply would not have had the equipment to magnify fibres in such detail that we could determine their type and even their colour. All in all, we would have been pretty much in the dark.

"But here we were, it was 1996, and in a short space of time we had learned that before this girl died of suffocation she had scratched or clawed at something that deposited *traceable* fibres under her nails. We knew that at some undetermined time prior to death she had engaged in sexual activity that had involved the depositing of semen in her mouth, anus and vagina.

"*And* we knew something else. The coldness of the water, and short lapse of time before the body was found, meant that genetic analysis of the semen deposits was possible, and had indeed taken place. We now knew that the semen in Ingrid Pereda's body had been put there by three different men. Their genetic profiles were now on record. We had provided the police with everything they needed to wreak havoc."

Inspector Vincente Serrano said that he felt the case was being solved backwards. So often, the burden of producing unassailable proof in a case of suspicious death comes after the police investigation and the pinpointing of suspects.

"Yet here I was, setting out to find my suspects, and already the whole scientific case against them, including their genetic profiles, was ranged and ready, lying at the disposal of the prosecution."

Serrano had the case sewn up inside two days. He interviewed Emilia Bazan, who gave him details of Ingrid's first boyfriend, Gabriel Borea. She also told him about Ingrid's apparent affair with Gabriel's father, Pascual Borea. That immediately rang a bell.

"We had had a complaint, eight months before," Serrano said, "about Signor Borea wining and dining an off-duty group of air stewardesses, then trying to coerce two of them into participating in an orgy, of sorts, at an apartment in the city. No case was made because the airline in question made the two stewardesses withdraw their complaint. By that time, we had done some digging and knew that this Borea was known in the red-light areas, and two females on the streets told us, independently, that he was always on the lookout for fresh young girls for himself and his friends."

From the description of the man with the bluish mouth described to them by Emilia, the police believed they knew who she meant: he was another cruiser on the vice scene, and when the records were checked it was noted that he was a business associate of Pascual Borea.

"The description of the soft-top Bentley was also fortuitous," said Serrano. "There was only one of that particular colour in Barcelona. We checked the records on the owner and found he had twice been cautioned for propositioning female minors. And yes, he was a known associate of Pascual Borea."

Inspector Serrano decided that the best plan of action would be to make a frontal assault on Pascual Borea. They found him in the office at his bottling plant.

"I waded straight in with a stunt that was technically very risky," Serrano said, "but on balance I was confident it would work, and I think my air of confidence was helped by the fact that Pascual looked scared behind the tight mouth and the steady stare. I know scared when I see it, no matter what it's hidden under."

Serrano told Pascual Borea that the police now knew the whole story of what happened to Ingrid Pereda. He had played on her innocence, seduced her and "broken her in," to use a phrase he was known to employ when talking about deflowering virgins. Then it was sharing time. He had shared her with his friends, and they had kept her sweet by treating her like a lady, on those occasions when they were not treating her like a sex toy.

"Your friends have admitted what happened the other night and they have given you up, Signor Borea. It was your fault the girl died, and they're prepared to testify to that in court."

The lie paid off. Borea lost control of himself. He screamed and shouted, knocked over his chair and kept pointing at the window, talking terrified gibberish. It was more than a minute before Serrano understood that Borea was trying to put the record straight. Finally, the detectives persuaded him to slow down and defend himself in terms that were comprehensible to ordinary human beings.

"He spilled everything," Serrano said. "They had been partying, he said, him and his grotesque buddies and Ingrid, who had been heavily dosed with cocaine to get her in the mood for the kind of excesses they had planned. He described the bizarre foursome that had culminated in Ingrid's death. In the heat of the action, with three men thrusting at her, she had appeared to slump. They carried on, unaware that anything was wrong. Afterwards, when they saw what they had done, they decided they had to get rid of the body."

"Whose car took her to the harbour?"

Borea admitted it was his.

"It has fawn carpet in the trunk?"

Borea thought about it, then nodded.

"We believe that fibres found quite deep under Ingrid Pereda's fingernails came from the trunk of your car," Lammas said. "We will check on that. In the meantime, you're under arrest."

The other two men were arrested later the same day. The fibres from the trunk of Borea's car were found to be a match for those taken from beneath Ingrid's fingernails.

"It could have meant, of course, that she wasn't dead when they put her in the trunk," Dr. Lammas said. "It might have been that she simply passed out from lack of oxygen, then came-to in the trunk, but was too weak to revive fully in that atmosphere. On the other hand it might have been a post-mortem spasm. Whatever happened, her fingertips had to press against the carpet with reasonable force to get the fibres so deeply under the nails. We don't really know the exact time or place of her death. All we know is, she had died by the time they threw her in the water."

Pascual Borea and his two associates were tried and sentenced to twenty years' imprisonment.

FOURTEEN

JEALOUS HEART

In May, 1983, members of a railway maintenance crew found the body of a woman inside a trackside hut at Woodhouse, near Wakefield in Yorkshire. She was young and attractive, dressed in a dark shirt, yellow sweater and high-heeled shoes. A forensic pathologist, Dr. Trevor Smith, was on the scene twenty minutes after the discovery of the body. He noted that although there was a tearing injury to the scalp at the back of the dead woman's head, there was no apparent fracture of the skull. There were various cuts and scratches on her face, legs and arms, but no superficial signs of an injury that might have killed her.

The body was eventually removed to the mortuary. An autopsy revealed that although there was only slight external damage to the head, the frontal lobes of the brain were virtually pulped. The finding was not unusual, Dr. Smith said. The woman had suffered what is known as a contrecoup injury.

"When the term contrecoup is used," Smith said, "it's nearly always in relation to brain damage. When a moving head hits the ground, or comes into contact with some other fixed surface, brain damage often occurs on the opposite side of the head from the point of impact. On the other hand, when a weapon hits a relatively motionless head, the brain damage happens right under the point of impact—that's called a coup injury."

The mechanism of contrecoup injury, Smith said, is still the subject of argument, but such things as rotational force, shearing stress and shock waves have all been blamed at one time and another.

"We often see contrecoup injury accompanied by a coup injury, that's not uncommon either, but in a lot of cases there's hardly any damage at the point of impact. Contrecoup damage happens when either the side or the back of the head hits an immovable object—the serious damage showing up on the opposite side of the brain from the point of impact—but it's practically unknown for a fall on the front of the head to cause a contrecoup injury in the back of the brain. Don't ask me why."

While the absence of contrecoup damage does not rule out the possibility of a fall on the head, its presence is practically certain proof that the deceased person's head was moving fast and was suddenly arrested by impact with something hard.

"So for the time being, we could assume that the dead woman on the table had died as the result of a fall on to the back of her head. We could also assume it didn't happen in the little hut where she was found. There was barely room for her in there, and the dirt and debris on the wound at the back of the head did not match any of the material the forensic team picked up at the hut. On the basis of that finding, it could be assumed also that the body had been moved to the hut after death had occurred."

Other findings at the autopsy were that the deceased had been smoking cannabis close to the time she died—the elements which cause euphoria, called tetrahydrocannabinols, were detected in the saliva, in the urine and on the tissues of the lips and mouth. There was also a quantity of semen in the vagina.

Photographs of the woman were circulated and eventually she was identified as the wife of John Eldridge, 34, a police constable from Wakefield, who reported that his wife Pat, 28, had been missing from home for two days.

"Around the time John Eldridge was making a formal identification of the body," Dr. Smith said, "another body was found near Normanton, which is several miles northeast of the place where Pat Eldridge was found. This was the body of a man, and I went out there to have a look. He was thirtyish, well groomed as far as I could tell, wearing a navy-blue Hugo Boss jacket, light grey trousers and good Italian shoes. His neck was broken and the top of his skull was fractured. There was no identification on the body, which was lying on the bank of a stream on the outskirts of town."

The autopsy on the man showed, predictably, that he had died from the combined effects of severe brain injury and a broken neck. A photograph was circulated and within hours he was identified as Steve Prout, an unmarried sales representative from Leeds.

"Apart from the fact that Pat Eldridge and Steve Prout appeared to have been dead for approximately the same length of time, we had no special reason to see a connection in the deaths. Our main concerns lay elsewhere—for instance, we wanted to establish whose semen was in Pat's body when she died, but we were reluctant to ask her husband about it, largely because for two days prior to discovering his wife was gone, he had been away on picket control—it was at the time of the coal miners' strike—so there was scarcely a chance he had been the last one to have sex with her."

A connection was made between the deaths of Pat Eldridge and Steve Prout when a forensic technician established that dirt on Prout's jacket was of the same composition as traces lifted from Pat's skirt and sweater. Another peculiar linking factor was that the soles of their shoes both had flinty particles of black volcanic ash embedded in the soles.

"It was the kind of stuff imported as bricks from the Canary Islands," the technician said. "It's used a lot for garden edging and on ornamental walls and patios."

With the link established, Dr. Smith's first move

was to compare Steve Prout's semen with that found in Pat Eldridge. They were not the same.

"So there was a third man somewhere in her life," he said, "unless by some outside chance that was her husband's semen we found in her. There was nothing else for it, now. We would have to talk to him about it."

Detective Sergeant Alec Young interviewed John Eldridge at home. He explained about the apparent connection between Pat's death and that of Steve Prout.

"I asked him if he knew Prout," Young said, "and he just stared at me, then he said, 'Are you telling me my wife knew this man?' I said I wasn't sure, I couldn't be sure, given the inconclusive evidence.

"He told me I was talking nonsense. I repeated that I was only following a line of enquiry, I hadn't said the two were acquainted, but he was getting hot in the neck now, imagining God knows what, and I thought great, he's getting riled up already, and I haven't even hit him with the other bit yet. So I let him fume at me for a while, then I asked him bluntly when he had last had sexual intercourse with his wife. Boy, that did it."

John Eldridge was furious with the detective. He demanded to know what relevance a question like that could have, what right a detective thought he had to ask such things. He said he had a good mind to call Detective Sergeant Young's superior and lay a formal complaint.

"I was patient with him, his life had just been

turned upside down after all, and I was here to make the chaos worse. I told him about the semen being found in Pat's body. This time he looked like I'd knifed him—mouth shut, eyes wide, breathing kind of strained. Then at last he said, 'There's got to be a mistake here.' And I thought, I could go on for hours, making it as easy for him as possible, playing down the obvious, but I didn't have time for that. I only had to think of the pile of paper on my desk. I wasn't a social worker, I reminded myself, I was an over-worked copper.

"I went straight to the core reason for my visit. I told him there was no mistake, Pat had semen in her vagina when she was found. Tests had already determined it didn't belong to Steve Prout, so we would now need a sample from John Eldridge."

The direct approach worked. Eldridge stopped protesting and simply nodded. He said he would drop the specimen in at the forensic lab the following day. Before Young left, he told Eldridge it would be necessary to make a thorough search of the house. Eldridge nodded again and let Young show himself out.

The specimen of semen from John Eldridge did not match that from his wife's body. No one on the case had expected it would.

Meanwhile, a forensic technician assisting on the search of the Eldridge house decided he would prise the snug-fitting plastic frame from around a travel mirror. He explained later that it was the kind of thing he always did on a house search.

"People will conceal pictures or documents in tight

or narrow spaces that look as if they would hide nothing," he said. "It's not just an expedient, either. The desire to conceal by cunning is bedded deep in many people. They will hide things down the backs of picture frames and in the spines of books, when there are many more convenient and secure places the stuff could be put. It's a human peculiarity that I always remember, and you'd be surprised the amount of evidence I've dug out of picture frames and CD cases and countless other tight places over the years."

When the technician opened the back of the mirror he found two strips of photographs, the kind produced by do-it-yourself booths in stations and department stores.

"One strip showed Pat Eldridge smiling cheek-to-cheek with Steve Prout," said Detective Sergeant Young. "So now there was no doubt of a connection between the two. In the other strip, the pictures were posed identically to the first lot, except the man was different. He was about the same age as Prout, with fair hair and a wispy moustache. I got a copy made of the picture, isolating the unknown man, and had duplicates distributed among the troops."

At this point the police did not know what kind of case they were engaged upon. There was a strong probability of murder—the separation and concealment of the two bodies pointed strongly in that direction—but the scientific and medical evidence could as easily indicate accidental death in both cases.

"Neither body looked as if it had been attacked," said Dr. Smith. "The cuts, scratches and bruises were consistent with the deceased having fallen, there was nothing we could justifiably add to that. So the thrust of the police enquiries was somewhat blunted, because they didn't know if they were looking for someone guilty of doing more than hiding a couple of bodies. The police are only ever at their best when they know what they're chasing."

On a visit to the Eldridge house to ask John Eldridge more questions about his wife's known acquaintances, Detective Sergeant Young was stopped on his way there by a woman at the house opposite.

"He's out," she told Young. "Perhaps I can be of some help to you?"

Young asked her how she thought she might help.

"I used to see Pat's boyfriend coming and going," she said. "My name's Jane, by the way, Jane Loudon."

She invited Young into the house and made him a cup of coffee. He asked her why she hadn't given a statement to the police when they made house-to-house enquiries the day after the dead woman was identified. She was away, she said, and had in fact only returned home the evening before, but she had already heard all about the Eldridge girl being found dead.

"Hardly surprises me," she told Young. "Women who behave like she did, they always run the risk of something extreme happening to them."

Young produced a pocket tape recorder and asked Jane if she would mind talking to him about Pat Eldridge's behaviour. She didn't mind at all.

"Pat was always flighty," Jane said. "They've lived over there two years, and I remember in the first six months, she was over-familiar on several occasions with my late husband. He died a year ago, a stroke, very sudden. Anyway, Pat Eldridge's husband has always worked a lot of overtime, he's that sort of chap, stodgy, regular, industrious—and that gave her a lot of time to herself. Except she didn't stay by herself for long. Friends of mine would see her in town, in the wine bars, talking to men—she was seen in the local Chinese place more than once with different men. I know there are a lot of silly fickle married women about, but what she was doing was just a bit too bold for a policeman's wife."

Then, about six months ago, Jane said, Pat Eldridge took the even bolder step of having a man visit her at home.

"He would leave his car at the foot of the hill and walk up the avenue—as if that would fool anybody."

Young showed her a picture of Steve Prout and asked if that was the man. No, Jane said, he looked nothing like that. Young showed her the picture of the fair-haired man with the moustache.

"You've got him," Jane said. "That's the very chap. Drives a black Ford Granada."

Jane had no idea what the man's name was. "But he was her regular comforter."

Other women on the street had said they thought there was another man. Jane was the only one who admitted to having seen him. Before Young left, he asked her to look at the picture of Steve Prout again.

She took it to the window and stared at it for nearly a minute. "No," she said finally, "I'm sorry, I don't think I've ever seen him before."

Meanwhile the forensic scientist who found the photographs had been examining the marks on the clothes again and had found yellow deposits on the woman's yellow sweater. The marks were camouflaged at first because of the similarity to the shade of the garment. The deposit, which looked like a powdery paint, was transferred to a specimen bottle and sent to the analytical laboratory for a priority evaluation.

The results were back in three hours. The yellow deposit had been analysed as an exterior wall paint, quite freshly applied.

Paint dealers and suppliers were contacted. Over a three-day period sixty constables showed the specification and a colour specimen card to almost a hundred suppliers throughout the region. One man, with premises on an industrial park near Bradford, remembered the batch—he had made it up specially, because the customer's wife had wanted something to offset the blue flowers she grew in the border around the house. The supplier looked up the customer's name and address and gave them to the police officer.

"The name was Mark Rudland," Young said. "I borrowed a forensic technician from the lab, then we got in the car and drove out to the house, which was on the moors. It was a pretty place, set in a hollow at the top of a steep winding drive."

The house, Young noted, was definitely reminiscent of the colour of Pat Eldridge's sweater. It was a vivid canary yellow that did, indeed, offset the blue flowers in the border.

Mark Rudland was not at home, but his wife was.

"She was nervous of us, I think," Young said, "but she wasn't hostile. I explained I'd like to come back and talk to her husband, but in the meantime, would she mind letting a forensic technician take a tiny scraping from a portion of the newly-painted house, at a spot where it wouldn't show? She told us to go ahead."

Back at the lab, the particles of stone powder mingled with the paint were found to match perfectly the particles in the paint found on Pat Eldridge's sweater.

"So I went out to the house again," Young said, "armed with a new wedge of certainty and accompanied by a detective constable. This time Mark Rudland was at home. His black Granada was parked in front of the house. The second I set eyes on him I could see he was the man in the pictures—fair-haired, with a wispy moustache. I could also see he was ready for me, all tensed and defensive.

"I asked him if he would mind answering a few questions. He responded by asking me who the hell I thought I was, coming up to his house while he was away, intimidating his wife and cutting great chunks out of the paintwork?"

Young remained calm. He assured Rudland there had been no intention to intimidate, and the tiny speck of paint that was scraped off was needed for a comparison test in the laboratory, in connection with traces that had turned up in a case under investigation.

Then Young asked Rudland if he knew Pat Eldridge. No, he said, the name meant nothing to him. Young said there were people prepared to say that Rudland not only knew Pat Eldridge, but that he had on several occasions visited her at home.

"He denied it again," Young said. "He got very agitated, saying I was trying to involve him in something he knew nothing about."

As they stood on the doorstep arguing, the detective constable noticed that the wall at the foot of the garden was topped with volcanic brick.

He went down across the lawn and looked. The wall was about six feet high, but the drop on the other side was nearer forty feet, into a rocky ravine. Using his initiative—and knowing Detective Sergeant Young would not like to be interrupted while he was working on a suspect—the detective constable used his radio to call the station and ask a detective there to alert the forensic team, who might care to come out and have a rummage down in the rocky ravine behind the wall.

Back at the house Mark Rudland continued to argue that he knew nothing about any woman by the name of Pat Eldridge. Young finally took out a picture of Rudland and Pat, cuddling and smiling. Rudland looked at it, his mouth churning. He said nothing more. He simply shrugged.

Young took Mark Rudland away for questioning. An hour later a forensic team examined the ravine on the other side of the Rudlands' wall and collected earth samples. One of them found a dried mark on a rock that could have been blood.

Back at the station Rudland was put in a cell to stew for a while, and to allow time for the samples from the ravine to be brought back and evaluated in the laboratory.

"The forensic people worked like beavers," Young said. "It would have been perfectly fitting if, after all their work, one of them had been handed the job of going into the interview room and mopping the floor with Rudland. They had made the case, no question of that. We'd have had nothing without them, but in the scheme of things, the razzmatazz and the moments of good theatre fall to the likes of me, so, when a good set of interim results was to hand, and we'd got together a summary of all the evidence, I went to talk with our suspect."

Young sat opposite Mark Rudland in the interview room and told him he would ask no more questions. He simply wanted Rudland to hear the evidence that had been assembled.

"First of all," Young said, "there are photographs proving that you and the dead woman were intimately acquainted. An eyewitness can put you at the Eldridge house, on several occasions. Traces of exterior wall paint found on Pat Eldridge's sweater match exactly the new paint on the outside of your house, right down to the stone-dust component."

At this point, Young noticed, Rudland had the classic breathless, bewildered look of the felon smothering under the weight of evidence he either overlooked or never imagined could exist. Young pressed on.

"The earth on Steve Prout's clothes and shoes came from the same source as the traces on Pat Eldridge's skirt and shoes—specifically, it came from the ground at the bottom of a ravine, which lies behind the wall at the bottom of your garden, Mr. Rudland. Also, traces of the man's blood were found on a rock down there. We intend to get an order demanding a specimen of your semen to compare with seminal fluid found in Pat's body. You needn't comply with the order, of course, but I've found a refusal lets a jury draw the appropriate conclusion.

"Finally, Mr. Rudland, there is evidence to suggest, strongly, that both Steve Prout and Pat Eldridge stood on the wall at the bottom of your garden just prior to their death."

There was so much circumstantial evidence, Young told Rudland, that they could get him put away without a statement.

"You should bear this in mind, however. If you refuse to tell anyone what happened, the judge will probably hit you with the worst punishment he can legally muster, out of spite."

Rudland asked if he could have a cup of tea. When it was brought, he said he had decided to tell Young what had happened.

"I found out about this other man in Pat's life," he said. "That was what started it. She and I, we had a good thing going; I couldn't see any likelihood that it would end, not unless I did something deliberately to finish it. I even thought I had covered myself if anything did go wrong—she'd promised me she destroyed the kiosk pictures of her and me, that was one of the loose ends. I never imagined she hadn't destroyed them, just like I never believed she'd cheat on me."

Young was tempted to remark that if she was already cheating on her husband, there was no credible obstacle to her doing it on Rudland. But he said nothing. Rudland was on a confessional flow.

"I actually saw her with this man, this Steve Prout," Rudland said. "I was enraged. There's no other word for it. I was half out of my head with jealousy. Once I'd caught on I followed them around—eventually I even knew where they parked to have sex."

One night when he could take it no longer, he said, he took his pistol and went to where they would park. He arrived early and as soon as they stopped got in the car: he knew it wouldn't be locked, because Pat had a terror of being burned alive in a car and insisted the doors never be locked.

"I was incredibly tense," he said. "Excited, too. I was all nerves, all responses. The inside of the car stank of cannabis, they had been smoking a joint. I hit Prout on the head with the gun and dragged Pat into the back of the car. I had sex with her, then when Prout came round I made him drive at gunpoint all the way back to my house. My wife was away, I've got no neighbours, so they could make all the noise they wanted, it would make no difference.

"It was late in the evening but there was still some light. I got the stepladder and made them stand on the wall. Truth was I wanted to shoot them, but this was better. I gave them the option of jumping down into the ravine or being shot. I said I would count to three . . .

"Then Pat did something, I don't know what; it was fright I think, an involuntary movement. Anyway she fell backwards. Prout watched her go, he looked helpless, then we heard her hit the bottom and he shouted at me and called me a twisted bastard. I was furious. I raised the gun, I was really going to shoot him, but he turned and jumped off the wall, straight into the ravine."

Rudland said he waited to hear if there were any sounds from the ravine. There were none. He got his wife's Land Rover, picked up the bodies and dumped them miles away. Leaving them at separate locations was something he couldn't explain.

"I wanted to dissociate myself from the deaths, and I suppose I wanted to dissociate them from each other . . ."

Following a short trial, Rudland was sentenced to two terms of life imprisonment. Pat Eldridge's husband, John, resigned from the police and shortly afterwards formed an attachment with Mark Rudland's wife. A year after Rudland was imprisoned his wife's petition for divorce was granted. She married John Eldridge and moved with him to the north of France, where they eventually bought a farmhouse and set up a successful business importing and selling English cheese.

FIFTEEN

MISSING

On the western edge of St. Louis, Missouri, is Forest Park, where visitors will find the St. Louis Zoo and the St. Louis Art Museum, which houses one of the world's outstanding collections of German Expressionist paintings. Elsewhere in the park there are pleasant walkways, an educational centre and a children's play area with swings, slides and a roundabout.

On a sultry July morning in 1987, Axel Sawyer sat on a bench among the other parents, leafing through his newspaper while a few yards away the children played. On the bench next to Axel's a man swatted at a bee that hovered too near his head. It swerved away, buzzing close to Axel, who flapped at it with his newspaper. He looked at the other man and grinned, then glanced across at the play area. His smile faded. He looked from the swings to the slides, then to the roundabout.

"David?"

Axel stood up, dropping his newspaper.

"David!"

He ran to the swings, looked behind a climbing frame, ran back to his bench.

"My little boy," he said. Several anxious adult faces turned towards him. "David, my little boy—he's gone."

An impromptu search began. Axel, three other fathers and four mothers set out across the park, calling David's name. A woman asked what he looked like and Axel told her—fair hair, big blue eyes, a four-year-old in jeans and a green T-shirt. The description spread among the searchers and others joined in. After ten minutes somebody suggested they tell the police.

An hour-long search by parents, park staff and police officers produced no sighting of little David Sawyer. They searched the park and the surrounding streets, twice, and then the police told Axel the matter would have to be treated as an abduction. Axel stood taking that in, then he broke down in tears.

"What I can't shake," he told a female officer at the police station, "is the way it all started out so fine, such a real nice morning, a perfect day for the park. One bad moment changed it—if I'd taken him there later, or earlier, or if I'd been watching him more, the day would have stayed nice, life would have stayed nice instead of this . . ."

The officer told him it was natural to blame himself

and it was just as natural to think "what-if"; he should try to keep a good attitude, she said, he should hold the thought that police and auxiliaries were out looking everywhere for young David. Meantime, Axel could help by letting them have a few details for the record.

He was 27, he told them, currently unemployed, but with good prospects because he was an excellent carpenter. His wife Denise was at her mother's in Kansas City, because the old lady was asthmatic and she'd had a bad turn three or four days ago. Axel had been looking after their only child David on his own, because Denise couldn't take him with her to Kansas. His mother-in-law had an aversion to young children, who always made noise and mess, according to her, and brought on her asthma even worse than usual.

Later that day, when David still hadn't been found, three detectives accompanied Axel Sawyer back to his home.

"You mustn't get offended," Detective Murray Busch told him. "We have to close off all the areas of possibility, and one of them gets closed off good and hard once we've searched the house. You understand, don't you?"

Axel said he did, he understood that they had to assume the worst about everybody and work upwards from there.

"The house was tidy enough," Murray Busch said afterwards. "It was clean too, I suppose, although the general impression we got was that the Sawyers didn't care much about the place. It had a kind of seedy look.

One of my officers found the kid's diapers in a wash pail, and he was surprised, because this kid was four years old, and still he was using diapers. The smell of ammonia when he lifted the lid of the pail was pretty strong, too. But we had to remind ourselves this was a guy coping with a kid on his own—they don't have the instincts women have, they don't know how to set up good routines."

No trace of the child was found at the house. On the way out Detective Busch saw a woman watching from a neighbouring house and he stopped to talk to her. He asked if she knew the Sawyers and their little boy. She said she certainly did. The little boy David was kind of a cry-baby for his age, but that wasn't abnormal she supposed with a mother like that.

"Like what?" Busch said.

"Domineering," the woman said. "She's not cruel to the baby or anything, but she shouts at him too much, and she shouts at her husband all the time. He's real henpecked, that Axel, but you won't say I said so, will you?"

Busch promised he would keep the information to himself.

"When I got back to the station I sat and thought about the case for a while," Busch said, "and I decided we'd have a better picture of that household if we got a forensic slant on it. I called Forensic Services and asked if a team could go out there and do a sweep. Then I called Axel and told him the men in white suits would be over, but he wasn't to worry about that, it was routine."

Axel did worry about it and he turned up at the station next morning and demanded to know what they thought he was guilty of. People were sifting the dust on his floors, he told a female detective, and other people were taking samples of water from the wash pail and pulling stuff out of the drain in the sink. Just what the hell was going on?

"If you want to accuse me of something, then please do it, but cut out all this pussyfooting around without saying what's really on your mind."

When Busch showed up, Axel pounced on him. He demanded to know what had prompted such a thorough examination of his home. He also wanted to know if a similar amount of energy was going into the search for his son.

"Well now I was really beginning to think something *was* wrong," Busch said. "Here was this allegedly henpecked man sounding off like a drill sergeant and refusing to accept that the elimination of suspects is a standard police procedure. I've seen plenty of worried people in similar circumstances, I've seen them get mad, too, but not like this.

"For one thing, the level of anger didn't seem to suit Axel's personality. For another, he was displaying anger and nothing else—no anxiety, not a sign of worry. I guess what I thought I saw was an act being performed by somebody who had never done it before, a guy who should have put in a lot of rehearsal time before he tried it out in public."

Denise Sawyer returned to St. Louis twenty-four hours after her son had disappeared. She showed every symptom of anxious motherhood, and where her husband had shouted mere complaint at the officers, Denise shouted her fear and her anxiety and her lack of faith in the police system.

"My child is missing!" she yelled at Busch, as if he didn't know. "He's been taken! What's being done about it? Can you imagine what it's like? I'm terrified to imagine anything about him, I can't even picture his little face without thinking somebody's doing something horrible to him!"

Busch did his diplomatic best and brought in an experienced female officer to try to contain Denise Sawyer's distress. He also noticed that throughout his wife's harangue, Axel had stood silently by, nodding agreement, making scarcely a sound.

"The neighbour was right," Busch said. "Axel was pussy-whipped. I was convinced now that his anger was all a cover-up for something I didn't want to define too sharply, just yet."

Busch went into a huddle with the forensic people. They told him that although all the test results were not yet in, they could give him a troubling fact or two. To begin with, the faeces and urine on the diapers in the bucket were several days old. No diapers were found that had been more recently soiled. Traces of baby cereal and other obvious children's food were found in the drain and that, too, was several days old.

"Little David still used a bottle of milk with a teat," a chemist said. "We found two cleaned bottles and one with dregs of milk in it, standing on the cabinet by David's bed. The milk was several days old. In short, we couldn't find a trace of the child that was any less than four, at best three, days old."

"And we have a suggestion," said a forensic technician. "You should get a look at the security tapes from the cameras outside the museum at Forest Park."

Busch hadn't known there were security cameras in that location. Neither had any of the other officers in his team.

"They're a condition of the insurance cover," the technician said. "Strictly speaking they're intended to watch the entrances, the exits and part of the perimeter, but I had a look yesterday on my way home—one of the cameras isn't at such a steep angle as the others. I bet it looks right over into the play area."

"What do you think I might find, if I get a look at the tapes?" Busch asked.

"What we bet you *won't* find," the technician said, "is a picture of young David Sawyer."

Busch visited the museum later that day and was told that Camera 6, the one that took in a wider view than the others, did look into the play area. It was not an intentional arrangement; the camera had become misaligned during structural work and although there were plans to reposition it, no one was in any hurry, since the administration felt there were already too many cameras watching the outside of the museum.

The tapes from Camera 6 for the day when David Sawyer was alleged to have disappeared were located and Busch and two other detectives sat down in a viewing room to watch them.

"It's always a dreary job," said Busch. "We watched

people come and go, right from the time the gates opened. We even caught sight of a known paedophile hanging around by the swings, but he went away again when a belligerent-looking park attendant stopped and stared at him.

"We saw the parents start to turn up singly, in pairs and in little groups with their offspring. That went on for more than an hour and I was tempted to do a fast forward, but it was important to miss nothing.

"At 11:28am by the digital clock on the tape, we saw Axel Sawyer appear. We ran back the tape to just before he appeared in shot at the main gate, then ran it forward again. He was definitely alone. We watched him walk over to the play area slowly, keeping near the hedgerow, slipping on to the edge of a bench and insinuating himself into the scene without attracting attention.

"We sat and watched him do his act, going into the charade of losing David, doing his anguished father bit. The scumbag got all those people helping him, running around the place frantic, and there was never any kid there in the first place."

While Busch waited for the rest of the results from the forensic team, he decided he would talk to Denise Sawyer. Above all, at that time, he wanted to know as much as he could about Axel, and he wanted to be completely sure that Denise had no part in whatever had been done to David.

"She was aggressive, like before," he said, "but she was a lot more worried now and her resistance didn't have the spring in it like last time. I let her accuse me and the whole police department of doing nothing, of not doing enough, of not being properly aware of the kind of hell she was going through. When she slowed down some, I asked her what she thought of Axel, taking his attention off the kid the way he did, reading the paper when he should have been keeping an eye on David.

"She said he was a useless shit, always had been, and she planned to divorce him anyway. I asked her how long she'd planned to do that and she said months. She was taking the boy with her, she said, and then stopped, and she started to cry and right there I saw the difference, the authenticity of it, a bewildered scared parent, not wanting to confront all the terrible possibilities."

Busch let Denise cry for a while, then he got her some coffee, gave her a cigarette, and asked her to tell him all about the divorce plans. She appeared grateful to have someone in whom to confide.

"The reason I was away these few days," she told Busch, "was to see the man I plan to spend the rest of my life with. We've been making our plans and he wanted me with him to be sure I like the house he's buying, and the furniture, all that."

Busch asked where she had met the man.

"I've known him years, since I was a kid. I would have married him before if he'd asked me, but he was too young. He knew that and I should have known it too, but instead, when I realised he didn't want to settle down until he had a job and a real home, I went off and married Axel, just to have a husband. Can you imagine that? I paid for it, mind. I got what I had coming. I'm not telling you anything I didn't tell Axel when I say he's a worthless bastard. He'd sooner lie on the couch than do anything. He hates any kind of work, and he's a chronic liar—he'd tell a lie even when the truth would sound better. That's the prince I married."

Denise stopped talking suddenly and gulped her coffee. Then she looked at Busch and asked him if he thought Axel had done something to the baby.

"Do you think he's capable of harming David?" Busch said.

"Anything negative, I think he could do it. I already asked him to tell me straight, did he do something bad, and he went all hysterical like a girl and swore to me that David disappeared in the park, that it happened exactly the way he said. I don't know if I believe him or not."

Busch was sure he believed Denise. He was sure now that she had no part in Axel's deception.

"I had two of my men bring Axel in for more questioning. I didn't want to show him our hand, not yet, not until we had everything that forensics could give us. What I wanted was to see how well he could hold out after all this time, and I also hoped to weaken a few of the strands in his resistance."

Axel looked cagey this time, Busch said, as if he suspected the police knew things they were not telling.

"I asked him to tell me, honestly, if he had any idea what had happened to his son. He responded by demanding to know what that bitch had said. I asked him, deadpan, what bitch he was talking about. His wife, of course, he said, she'd been treating him strangely, as if she didn't believe his story about what happened to David.

"So I said to him, why don't you tell us right now what did happen? Well, Axel went mad, or he did a good job pretending. He punched the table and screeched at me that I was a sadist, treating him like this when he was torn apart over what happened to his son, over what some pervert might be doing to him right that minute."

After an hour Busch let Axel go home again. At nine that same evening Dr. Don Hagan, superintendent of the forensic services department, brought along the full results from the sweep carried out at the Sawyer house. *Almost* the full results, he corrected himself: a dark afterthought had meant that another series of tests were being carried out on an item taken from the garbage. The result should be in some time the following day.

"The facts he gave me were grim and kind of puzzling," Busch said. "I had to do some checking before I could feel comfortable hitting Axel with the whole payload of what we knew, so I decided to do my checking that night, then haul him in first thing in the morning."

Axel was brought to the police station at eight the following morning, bleary and unshaven. He started shouting as soon as Busch appeared, accusing him of playing the big tough cop to cover the fact he'd still got nowhere in the search for David.

"Sit down and shut your mouth," Busch told Axel. "There are a few things I want to tell you." He opened a folder on the desk in front of him. "First of all, I want you to know, Axel, that we know you didn't take David to the park that morning. You were picked up on a surveillance video, entering the park alone. Next, we know, from evidence at your home and from diligent questioning of your neighbours, that David had not been seen for three days prior to you saying he had disappeared.

"Forensic examination of your house revealed a smear of blood on the food tray of David's high chair which is consistent with his blood group as entered on his record at the Child Health Care Clinic."

Axel made to interrupt at that point and Busch told him to shut up. A detective tapped at the door, leaned in and put another folder on the table. "Final result from forensic," he said.

Busch read it quickly. He had to read it again to be sure he understood.

He continued reciting the facts to Axel. "The forensic team lifted a number of hairs from your living room. They turned out to be dog hairs, and one of the technicians had the initiative to check around the area and see if there were any dogs being kept nearby. Well you don't need me to tell you, Axel, that a very nasty Dobermann lives next door to you, and this morning I was able to determine that on occasion it has got through the fence and entered your house.

"Also found on your floor, on some parts of the upholstery of the couch, and on a chair, were traces of blood. Washed away, as far as the naked eye could see, but present nevertheless, and fully capable of being analysed. Again, the blood matches that of young David."

Busch paused and looked at Axel. His hands were clenched on the edge of the desk and he was staring fixedly at his knuckles.

"There was other stuff on the carpet and upholstery, and around the rim of the sink in the kitchen," Busch said. "It was identified as fat. Human fat."

Busch sat back, closed the folder and drew the new folder towards him. "And now there's this. The forensic lab tells me that material taken from the trash in a sack at the rear of your house was analysed yesterday, and it was found to be fragmented human bone."

Busch pushed both folders to one side and leaned forward sharply. "You'll never walk away from this," he told Axel. "It's too much. One way or another you're in over your shoulders. I would advise you to tell me what happened to your son. If you don't, I'll make up a story to fit the facts and I'll use it to bury you."

Axel started to sob. Again Busch told him to shut up. "Just tell me, Axel, and don't waste any more of my time."

"It was the dog," Axel said.

"Your neighbour's Dobermann?"

"Yeah, Jasper. He got into the kitchen while I was

upstairs; he could sometimes get through the fence. I tried to keep the loose slat hammered into place but it would come loose from time to time. So he got in, and the first thing I heard was David screaming. I ran downstairs and the dog had him on the floor; it had him by the back of the neck and it was shaking him. There was blood everywhere and when I hit Jasper with a broom he dropped David and grabbed him again, by the shoulder, and there was more blood and more shaking and the animal was like something crazy. I hit it between the eyes with the broom and it backed off, ran into the yard.

"I kicked the door shut and went to David. I can't tell you how bad it was. He was mutilated—his face was all torn, he had lost an eye. His chest was wide open. He just lay there moaning, his legs twitching. I thought, Christ, Denise will go crazy, she'll make my life hell for this."

Axel buried his face in his hands. Busch told him to go on.

"I stood looking at him, seeing all the injury, the unbelievable mess the dog had made of him, and I thought about Denise again, screaming at me, blaming me, never letting up . . .

"I went to the closet in the hall and pulled out my axe. I went back to the living room. David was still moaning and twitching, all horrible and bloody. I hit him once with the axe, hard, on the head. He still moaned and then I started chopping and chopping at him and when I knew he was dead I still went on chopping, breaking him into pieces. Then I let Jasper back in."

Busch stared at him. "You fed him to the dog?"

"I didn't have to do anything. Nothing would have stopped him." Axel paused, lit a cigarette. "When he was through, there wasn't much left. Not so much mess on the floor, either. I flushed what I could down the toilet, I threw some stuff in the trash, cleaned the place up . . ."

"And after a couple of days you went out and pretended David had been abducted."

"If he'd lived," Axel said, "his life would have been a misery. So would mine."

Later that day Denise Sawyer was told what had happened to her son. She became hysterical and had to be sedated. Later she told Busch that if she ever got a chance she would kill Axel.

"I told her I didn't think she would get a chance."

Axel Sawyer was tried for the murder of his son and was sentenced to 35 years' imprisonment, with no right to consideration for parole for at least twenty years.

SIXTEEN

PYRO

In the late fifties," said Tony Rogan, an 82-year-old former detective with the LAPD, "detective squads and forensic teams—they were called science-lab technicians then—usually worked as a unit. Detectives wore the hats and did the upfront questioning and swaggering, and behind us the sinister, all-knowing lab guys in the buff coats did obscure things with their mysterious instruments."

"We people on the crime detection side thought we were pretty sophisticated," said Phil Hanna, 83, who partnered Rogan for eight years prior to their retirement in 1965. "*And* our science lab hot-shots had the equipment to prove it. I remember there was a lot of chrome around, enough chrome to blind you if you didn't wear sunglasses—which we all did back then, anyway."

Rogan said, "He's right about the chrome. The lab guys had these chrome instruments that rattled very importantly. They had nifty little chrome vacuum cleaners they used for picking up dust and fibres, they had chrome probes, chrome forceps, they even had chrome cases on the thermometers they shoved up dead people's asses. A bag of instruments finished in quality chrome was the mark of a serious investigative technician."

"The stuff was heavy, too," Hanna said. "They used to lug around these cases filled with gadgets that had really serious weight. Devices with eyepieces on them for looking at things close up, and wind-out steel tapes for measuring—for a while there was even a heavy steel dispenser that fed out a liquid white line for drawing around bodies. Lots of cameras, too, big Speed Graphics and Rolleiflexes, and tricky flood-lights with dimmers and filters for night-time illumination of crime scenes. The way I look at it now, we probably needed all that hardware to cover our ignorance."

Rogan and Hanna were brought together in 1997 to discuss a baffling case in which they were involved in 1957. At that time they worked homicide detail out of the West Hollywood station in Los Angeles.

"The star investigative performer on the case," said Rogan, "without a shadow of a doubt, was Nick Lub-bock. He didn't let contradictions or blind alleys deflect his straight-arrow approach. He knew that in spite of signs that said otherwise, where there was crime there was a clue, and he would never let up until he found it."

Nick Lubbock was a forensic technician with qualifications in chemistry, physics, and ballistics. In 1957 he was in charge of the Central LAPD laboratory, with only two years to go until retirement. His work by then kept him deskbound, but he would get out in the field whenever he could.

"Wild horses wouldn't have kept him away from the Rogers House tragedy," said Hanna. "Before the smoke had settled he was up there with his bags and bottles and tweezers, without being asked."

Rogers House had been erected as a home for retired silent-film performers, and was named after Will Rogers, whose estate provided the funds in 1940, five years after his death. On a July evening in 1957 the house caught fire. In spite of the efforts of firemen it burned to the ground, and seventeen of the residents died in the fire.

"Some of them never even made it out of their beds," Rogan said. "The fire just whipped through the building. It was helped by the draughts, what with it being a warm night and so many windows being open. The Fire Chief and everybody who examined the facts, with one exception, agreed it was just an awful thing to happen, but it was an accident, one of those things. They all thought that except Nick Lubbock. Nick thought it was arson."

Lubbock died in 1964, but he is well remembered

by former colleagues. "He really upset the Fire Chief over the Rogers Home blaze," said Lewis Rollins, a retired fireman. "Nick insisted that the focus of the fire was too small for it to have been an accident. The Chief said that was baloney, a cigarette butt can start a fire and that's small, too. Nick came right back and pointed out that a cigarette doesn't burn a hole half-way into an inch-thick plywood shelf. The heart of that fire, he said, was small and uncommonly hot. It was something *designed* to start a fire."

Tony Rogan said that Nick Lubbock made no head-way with the Fire Chief, who dismissed his theory as cranky nonsense, but Homicide Division was cautiously interested. They had worked with Nick for a long time and he had a good track record as a man whose hunches and theories paid off.

"Nothing was hidden from the guy," Rogan said. "One time, a bunch of us were in a club over near La Brea, and one of the cabaret acts was a mindreader. He did this stunt where he drew a circle on the centre of a sheet of notepaper, and he asked a lady in the audience to imagine it was the world. She was then to take the paper, still imagining the circle was the world, and she was to write in the middle of the circle the place in the world she would most like to visit. She was to do it while the mindreader had his back turned, then she was to fold the paper in quarters and hand it back to him.

"Nick Lubbock watched like a hawk. The performer took the folded paper, tore it in small pieces and threw them into this miniature brazier he had burning on the table. He turned to the lady and told her to concentrate on what she had written. Then he picked up a big notepad, stared at the blank top page for a second, then started to write. When he finished he put the pen back in his pocket. He asked the lady what place name she wrote. She told him 'New Zealand'. He turned round the pad and showed her. He'd written 'New Zealand' in big letters."

Rogan said Nick Lubbock was beyond reach for the rest of the evening. He was intrigued by the trick, he sat staring into space, trying to work it out. Mysteries of any kind fascinated him and held his attention until he had fathomed them.

"Two days later Nick walked into the homicide office, all smiles, and handed me a piece of paper with a circle drawn on it. 'You can do it?' I asked him. 'Watch me,' he said. And he did it. He went right through the routine exactly the way the mindreader did. He asked me to think of a place and write it in the circle. I wrote it down—Newark, just for laughs. Then I folded it in four and handed it back to Nick. He tore it up, dropped the pieces in an ashtray and set them alight with his lighter. Then he did the rubbing the chin bit, rubbing the forehead, and finally he started writing. When he was finished he showed me. 'Newark' it said."

Nick had gone through the moves of the routine at home, over and over, and the eighth or ninth time he looked at the torn pieces of paper, he found that the one on top, when it was opened out, was the centre of the sheet, and the written name was intact, even though to all appearances the paper had been torn up and the name with it.

"After that, it was a piece of cake," Rogan said. "He thumbed off that one piece of paper and kept hold of it as he threw the others in the ashtray. When he went to his pocket for the pen to write on the pad, he used his thumb to open the paper like a little umbrella, and brought it out in the palm of his hand, together with the pen. When he poised the pen over the pad to start writing, he could see the written name right there, nestled in the palm of his hand. When he finished writing, he ditched the pen in his pocket and the piece of paper with it. He finished clean and he'd performed a miracle.

"Except Nick wasn't interested in doing the miracle any more. He'd worked it out, and that was all he'd wanted. Now he could put it from his mind for good."

When Lubbock talked to the lieutenant in charge of Homicide Division, he emphasised, again, that the place where the fire in the Rogers Home started had been a point-source of intense heat. Whatever started the fire, it had been sitting on a shelf in an open common room, where several people were watching evening television. Therefore it was reasonable to assume, Lubbock said, that the fire was started by something that looked innocuous enough to be left in open view. Either that, or it was so small that it could be easily placed so that no one was likely to take notice of it, no matter how unusual it looked.

The lieutenant asserted that he was interested in pursuing any possibility that the Rogers Home fire was a criminal case. He asked Lubbock if he could work up some solid evidence, because, as matters stood, there was nothing suspicious enough to warrant an investigation.

"You had to hand it to our lieutenant," Phil Hanna said. "He knew damn well that Nick Lubbock couldn't leave a mystery alone. It was safe for homicide to do nothing at all until Nick came up with something we could hang an investigation on. Maybe Nick knew the lieutenant was stringing him along. Maybe he knew and didn't give a shit, because one way or another, he was going to get right to the bottom of that case and prove it was a criminal act, not an accident."

Lubbock promised he would put together the foundations of a case. All he asked was that from time to time, Homicide Division would give him a little backup. No problem, the lieutenant promised him.

Lubbock kept extensive notes of all the cases he worked on—the file on the Rogers Home fire is three inches thick. There are drawings of the burnt-out skeleton of the building, speculative sketches of the common room before the fire started, and estimations of how the blaze managed to spread so quickly to all three floors.

On page 35 of the notes he remarks: *Three similar occurrences unearthed at El Segundo.*

On a stretch of sandy beach at El Segundo in the south-west of Los Angeles, Nick Lubbock had his weekend retreat, a two-storey white clapboard house that doubled as his reference library and archive.

Books and technical records occupied the entire upper floor and attic; there was even an overflow section in the garage.

In the sprawling archive, Lubbock found three other cases of fires at retirement homes that had resulted in the deaths of residents. All three fires had been written off as accidents, but their features, to Nick, were alarmingly similar to those of the conflagration at the Rogers Home.

The first of the three, at San Diego, had killed nine people when the top floor collapsed on to the two floors below, the structure weakened by a fire in a well-ventilated common room on the second floor. The San Diego Fire Chief's notes made reference to a "small fire source, no more than an inch or so," and the presumption at the end of the report was that a lit cigarette had caused the tragedy.

The second case, on the outskirts of Palm Springs, concerned a single-storey "retirement lodge" designed to house a maximum of twenty old people with the money to afford luxurious care in their twilight years. A fire that started on the sun veranda burnt down most of the building within thirty minutes, killing ten people. As before, it was noted that the probable source of the fire was relatively small.

In the third case, a fire had spread through another retirement home, also near Palm Springs. On this occasion the spread of damage was assisted, catastrophically, by the fact that the flames engulfed a gasoline pump belonging to the property and blew up the underground tank. The emergency services dragged twenty-four charred bodies from the burned-out building. An insurance company's fire-examiner filed a report noting that the fire appeared to have started in the day lounge, where several people were having a post-lunch nap when the fire broke out. The inspector noted that because of the extreme damage it was hard to estimate the size or even the rough shape of the causative element. Nevertheless, it was his opinion, going on the evidence of intense charring on an otherwise lightly damaged shelf by a window, that the source was quite small, certainly not more than an inch in length.

"Nick buried himself for a month in that investigation," Rogan said. "He kept making trips out to the ruins of the Rogers Home, walking around it, making sketches, and one time even taking along a little model he'd made of the TV lounge, just to check the kind of prevailing winds they had up there, and how they would collide in a room with open windows on three sides."

At the end of his month of intensive investigation, Lubbock appeared at Homicide Division at the West Hollywood Police Station. He looked tired, but he looked triumphant, too.

"I think I've got it," he told the lieutenant in charge. "I went through all the factors that might be common to the Rogers Home and three others in California that burned down the same way. One identical factor crops up in all four at the time they burned."

Rogan said that Lubbock had deliberately waited then, trying to compel the lieutenant to press him to go on. "Nick liked that, he liked you to say, 'Aw come on, Nick, be a pal, tell us what you know . . .' but the lieutenant didn't bite; he had something else on his mind, so he just stared at Nick and waited. Nick shrugged and said, 'It's a member of staff.' "

Now the lieutenant did have to press Lubbock. He was hooked, he had to know. When Lubbock went quiet again the lieutenant told him testily to go on.

"Nick told him it was a trained geriatric nurse," Hanna said, "a woman called Mia Clark. She had been employed at all four homes at the time they burned down, and what made that fact even more suspicious, Nick said, was that at two of the places she used a different name. That was quite an achievement in itself, going through all those personnel records, then double-checking thoroughly enough to discover one of the staff had been using aliases."

If it had not been for the policy of taking Polaroid pictures of members of staff and keeping the photographs with the records, Lubbock told them, he might never have caught on.

"So how do you prove this Mia Clark had anything to do with the fires?" the lieutenant asked.

"You'll recall you promised me some backup," Lubbock said. "Well, now's the time I need it."

Detectives Rogan and Hanna were detailed to find Mia Clark and question her.

"Finding her took us four days," Hanna said. "She had a tricky system of mail delivery that pretty much kept her whereabouts a secret. Her box number was an agency that automatically sent on the mail to another box number, and that one sent it to another one, where the mail lay until she picked it up, from a lockup box among rows of others on Hollywood Boulevard. In the end, once we'd located the final mailbox, we just waited for her to show up and collect her mail. While we were waiting we alerted Nick Lubbock in case he wanted to tag along. He was with us within the hour."

Mia Clark was a stern-looking middle-aged woman with grey hair and the kind of large flyaway spectacles that were beginning to be popular at the time. Rogan, Hanna and Lubbock watched her open her mailbox, drop the letters into her bag, then walk smartly back to where she had parked her car.

"There was no sense picking her up there and then," Hanna said. "We still didn't know where she lived, and since any incriminating evidence might be at her home, we decided to follow her and introduce ourselves only after we were sure she had arrived at her own place."

Mia Clark made it difficult to follow her. For thirty minutes she drove south, out towards Lakewood, heading in the direction of Long Beach. Then she began to veer south-east, on long straight roads with few other cars in sight.

"We had to hang back about a mile," Rogan said, "otherwise she would have seen us. As it was, I couldn't be sure she hadn't seen us already. For all I knew, this ride out to the barren stretches south of Los Angeles was just something laid on to spite us."

Eventually, Mia Clark pulled in at a white bungalow with outbuildings, miles from the nearest house.

"We pulled our car up behind hers and got out," Rogan said. "By the time we got to the door she was standing there glaring at us, hands on hips, looking every inch the nurse from hell. I identified myself and the two others and asked if we might come in and ask her a few questions. She was reluctant, but she said OK, and we went in."

The house was well furnished and tidy, but Lubbock immediately noticed some incongruities, and later he told Rogan and Hanna. There were no pictures on the walls and no sign of a mirror. Lubbock's first thought, he joked, was that Mia Clark was a vampire.

"Afterwards, when Nick mentioned about there being no pictures and no mirrors," Rogan said, "I began to realise what a strange place that house was. Right out there in the heart of nowhere was an odd spot for a solitary woman to choose, and although the furnishings were nice and everything had a spotless look, it was spotless to the point of lifeless sterility. You couldn't imagine a normal life being lived in there.

"I came straight to the point," Rogan said, "because I could see we'd get nowhere being gentle with this one. She radiated hostility. I asked her if she was aware of the huge coincidence in her life, the fact she had worked at four different retirement homes that had all burned down within the space of eighteen months—and each time one burned, she had been a member of staff at the time."

Mia Clark responded bluntly. If they were going to

charge her with anything, she said, they'd better do it, or get the hell out of her house.

"That was when I improvised," Hanna said. "I'd always noticed that when criminals have got their defences worked out and nicely cemented in place, they'll show a detective the hardest face they've got. The one thing that can change that, the one ploy that makes them nervous and unsure of themselves is if you search the premises without them being able to watch you do it. No matter how well they may think they've covered their tracks, they all worry when you go on a tour of their home, looking for something to nail them with."

Hanna's improvisation was to produce an official-looking sheet of paper and wave it at Mia Clark. "We have a warrant to look around, ma'am."

It was a letter from the golf club where Hanna was a member, reminding him his annual fees were due. Mia Clark didn't question it.

"Go ahead," she said, and Hanna was gratified to see the self-assurance slip, if only a fraction.

As Lubbock and Hanna moved off into the hallway to start the search, Mia followed them. Rogan said it would help if she stayed there in the living room with him and answered a few questions.

"As soon as we were in the kitchen," Hanna said, "I turned to Nick and asked him if he had any idea what we were looking for. He said, 'Leave it to me,' and that's what I did. I just followed him round."

Superficially there was nothing unusual in the house. Mia Clark appeared to lead a Spartan existence with few luxuries or inessentials. Hanna and Lubbock moved through the kitchen to the bedroom and then the small dining room. In a sideboard drawer Lubbock found a cardboard box, roughly the size of a cigarette packet. Inside was a bottle of purple crystals, a small bottle of glycerine, a couple of headache capsules, and a pin.

"It was just a collection of odds and ends that you might expect to find in a nurse's bag, or lying about her house," Hanna said. "Lubbock identified the crystals by their chemical name—he told me that when they were dissolved in water, they made a mild astringent antiseptic. Nurses and doctors sometimes administered the solution as a douche for fungal conditions. We would have passed up the box and its contents, if we hadn't found another box with exactly the same contents in another drawer. Nick looked at me, raised his eyebrows, and pocketed the box. We finished the search without finding anything else."

Rogan, Hanna and Lubbock left the house as soon as the search was complete. All three were in no doubt that Mia Clark was a strange person. Lubbock did not know yet what to make of the duplicated boxes, but he said he would take away the one he had purloined and he would rack his brains until he found an answer, assuming there was one.

In the meantime, Rogan made extensive enquiries into the background of Mia Clark. Little was known about her in California, beyond an exceptional employment record, and the fact that she occasionally changed her name.

"But in Denver, Colorado, we hit pay dirt," Rogan said. "I had taken the trouble to circularise as many state law enforcement authorities as I could, and now I was so glad I'd done that. Back came this dossier on geriatric nurse Mia Clark, who had a history of mental instability and a two-year conviction for fire-raising at an old-people's home in Denver. Nowadays they'd catch on to an itinerant dipstick like her right away, but back then inter-state communications weren't so fast or thorough. According to the police notes, she had doused an empty bed with gasoline and was actually seen torching it by two patients she thought were asleep.

"So now we had her. We knew she was a fire-raiser, and according to the record it was something she just did because she had to. No rhyme, no reason. It remained, of course, for Nick to come up with the goods connecting Mia to the other fires by something a lot less slender than coincidence."

It was Nick Lubbock's long-time girlfriend, Linda Ashe, who explained what happened the night he finally worked out the significance of the contents of the cardboard box.

"Nick was sitting cross-legged on my carpet," Linda said, "his tongue sticking out from one side of his mouth, which was a thing he always did to aid his concentration. In front of him on the floor was a stiff cardboard box. He'd just emptied a couple of head-ache capsules into the box. He was filling one half of one empty capsule from a bottle of purple crystals.

" 'You've started pushing dope,' I said to him.

"He grinned at me. 'Nobody could get high on this,' he said, and he put the other half of the capsule in position.

"I asked him what it was. He liked to be asked about what he was doing. So he put the capsule with the purple crystals in it on one side and picked up the other one. 'Big secret,' he said. That meant I should shut up and watch. Nick had this little bottle of liquid—later he told me it was glycerine—and he put five or six drops into a half-capsule."

Linda sat, fascinated, and watched as the half-capsule with the glycerine inside was forced carefully over the end of the capsule with the crystals inside. When the fit was absolutely tight, Lubbock applied a tiny strip of adhesive tape around the margin where the two units met. He looked up and patted the floor beside him. "Sit down," he told Linda, "and I'll show you."

He put the capsule he had just completed on an ashtray. "It just lies there, right?" he said. "Nothing happens. It's safe, you could carry it around all day. But if you do this . . ." He picked up a pin from the cardboard box and pushed it through the end of the capsule containing the crystals and into the part holding the glycerine. When he withdrew the pin, Linda could see the liquid seeping among the crystals, turning them muddy brown. Nothing else seemed to be happening.

"So?" Linda said.

"So keep watching it." For another ten seconds nothing happened at all, then the capsule clicked.

"Now!" Lubbock said, and as if he had commanded it, a plume of thick white smoke issued from the punctured end of the capsule. There was a hiss, which became louder, and suddenly the whole thing turned blindingly white hot. Linda could feel the heat from where she sat several feet away. The capsule burned for about half a minute then died, leaving the ashtray scorched, a tiny black pea remaining where the capsule had been.

Nick smiled. "Some gadget, eh? The heat produced in that thing makes sure there's going to be a fire, Linda. It's one of the very best incineration devices I ever saw."

Later he explained to Rogan and Hanna that it was basic chemistry, but it used components that were individually so simple and so innocent that they were above suspicion.

"In the right combination of quantity, pressure and rate of mixture, they produce white heat," he said. "Fire on demand, seconds after the fire-raiser walks away."

Rogan asked him how he had thought of the device.

"It came to me half in sleep," Lubbock said. "I'm sure I saw something like it at school, using the gelatine capsule. I sat down and scribbled it in my notepad, so I wouldn't forget the set-up, then I made one. As soon as I emptied out those headache capsules, I knew somehow I was on the right track. The only thing I wonder about now, of course, is how Mia Clark knew about the device."

Just for once, Rogan and Hanna were in a position to grin smugly in the presence of Nick Lubbock.

"Nursing is a profession Mia took up for cover," Rogan told Lubbock. "She's fully trained and has qualifications that allow her to practise in just about every state, but nursing wasn't the first thing she trained for."

He made Lubbock wait, and finally Nick couldn't bear it. "So tell me—what did she do before?"

"She taught high school."

"And her speciality, before you ask," Hanna added, "was chemistry."

When the case against Mia Clark was put to her in the presence of her lawyer, she offered no defence. Through the lawyer she let it be known that she would make no statement of any kind—whatever the pressure, whatever the consequences.

"She was determined to stay silent," Rogan said, "and that's what she did. In court, the whole grisly story was recited and Nick's evidence was there to back it all the way. He was asked to demonstrate the incendiary device in court, and you could hear the intake of breath from the jury when that innocent-looking little capsule suddenly smoked and turned white hot."

One or two people, including Phil Hanna, were watching Mia Clark at that moment. "Her eyes were bright and glassy, like somebody with a fever," he said. "She stared at that thing burning there, stared at it until it fizzled out. Then she bowed her head and shut her eyes tight. I looked at her really hard, and I could see she was forcing herself to keep from laughing. I tell you, that was a profoundly crazy woman."

A psychiatrist attested that Mia Clark was mentally disturbed, but that she knew right from wrong, and was therefore not insane. Following a trial lasting less than a week, Mia was found guilty of murdering sixty people.

The judge called an adjournment until Monday morning, at which time he would pass sentence. On Sunday night, Mia was found dead in her cell. She had pulled all the buttons off her prison dress and crammed them down her throat, suffocating herself.

INDEX

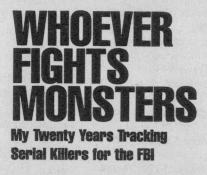

WHOEVER FIGHTS MONSTERS

My Twenty Years Tracking Serial Killers for the FBI

ROBERT K. RESSLER & TOM SHACHTMAN

He coined the phrase "serial killer", he advised Thomas
Harris on *The Silence of the Lambs*, he has gone where no
else has dared to go: inside the minds of the 20th century's
most prolific serial killers. From Charles Manson to
Edmund Kemper, follow former FBI agent Robert K.
Ressler's ingenious trail from the scene of the crime to the
brain of a killer in this fascinating true crime classic.

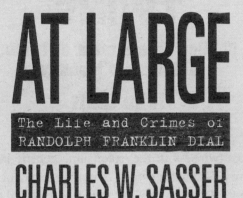